"For all who earnestly desire to grow in Christlikeness, *Uneclipsing the Son* is a must-read. In these stirring pages, Rick Holland reminds every believer of the most essential component for spiritual growth: a living, vibrant, dynamic relationship with the risen Lord, Jesus Christ. Simply put, this book is a soul-gripping charge and powerful call to singular loyalty and unwavering allegiance to the Son of God. But the Christian life is not simply *about* Christ, as this gifted author rightly notes; it is Christ *Himself.* This radiant Son must not merely have *a* place in our lives, but the unrivaled preeminence above all. I firmly believe that you will be both challenged and compelled by this book. But most of all, you will want to know Christ more deeply and follow Him more closely."

—STEVEN J. LAWSON, senior pastor,
Christ Fellowship Baptist Church, Mobile, Alabama

"Rick Holland is a gifted preacher, a faithful expositor, and he possesses a keen theological mind. His focus on the Christian life and the preeminence of Christ is both timely and truthful. Read it and pass a copy to a friend."

—DR. R. ALBERT MOHLER, JR., president,
The Southern Baptist Theological Seminary

"This book is an insightful, convicting reminder that no one and nothing other than Christ deserves to be the central theme of the tidings we as Christians proclaim."

—JOHN MACARTHUR, pastor-teacher,
Grace Community Church, Sun Valley, California

"It is possible to get so close to someone you no longer see them for who they are and what they are worth. Tragically, it is possible to do this with Jesus. Pastor Rick Holland brings us out of the shadows and into the glorious light of the Son of God as He is revealed in the Bible. Jesus is a great Savior who accomplished a great salvation for sinners. Perhaps it is time for you to get reintroduced to this great King. This book will help you do just that."

—DANIEL L. AKIN, president,
Southeastern Baptist Theological Seminary

"In this supremely helpful book, Rick Holland offers a wealth of biblical and practical help for keeping Christ at the center of our lives and in clear focus at all times. Whether you are just beginning your walk with Christ, struggling through the trials of spiritual adolescence, or a mature believer who disciples others, *Uneclipsing the Son* will give you a tremendous spiritual boost."

—PHIL JOHNSON, executive director, Grace to You

"If you want a snack, you will not find it in *Uneclipsing the Son*. If you want the food that leads to eternal life, welcome to a feast for your soul. I daily pray that I will know Jesus more clearly, love Him more dearly, and follow Him more nearly. This book comes as an answer to that prayer. May it be an answer to your heart's desire to know and love and follow the Savior who Rick Holland uneclipses before your eyes."

—DR. WILLIAM VARNER, professor of Biblical Studies,
The Master's College

UNECLIPSING
THE SON

RICK HOLLAND

KRESS
BIBLICAL
RESOURCES

UNECLIPSING THE SON
PUBLISHED BY KRESS BIBLICAL RESOURCES
PO Box 132228
The Woodlands, TX 77393

ISBN 978-1-934952-13-9

Cover design: John Martin
Interior design and typeset: Katherine Lloyd, The DESK

Printed in the United States of America
2011—First Edition

10 9 8 7 6 5 4 3 2 1

"Enjoy life with the woman whom you love all the days of your fleeting life which He has given to you under the sun; for this is your reward in life, and in your toil in which you have labored under the sun." (Ecclesiastes 9:9)

To Kim,
You are my reward.

Contents

Foreword

As Christians we have one message to declare: "Jesus Christ, and Him crucified" (1 Corinthians 2:2). "For we do not preach ourselves but Christ Jesus as Lord, and ourselves as your slaves for Jesus' sake" (2 Corinthians 4:5; cf. 1 Corinthians 2:2; Galatians 6:14).

Rick Holland understands that truth. This book is an insightful, convicting reminder that no one and nothing other than Christ deserves to be the central theme of the tidings we as Christians proclaim—not only to one another and to the world, but also in the private meditations of our own hearts.

Christ is the perfect image of God (Hebrews 1); the theme of Scripture (Luke 24); the author of salvation (Hebrews 12:2); the one proper object of saving faith (Romans 10:9-10); and the goal of our sanctification (Romans 8:2). No wonder Scripture describes the amazing growth-strategy of the early church in these terms: "They ceased not to teach and preach Jesus Christ" (Acts 5:42). That is the only blueprint for church ministry that has any sanction from Scripture.

The pastor who makes anything or anyone other than Christ the focus of his message is actually hindering the sanctification of the flock. Second Corinthians 3:18 describes in simple terms *how* God conforms us to the image of His Son: "And we all, with unveiled face, *beholding the glory of the Lord,* are being transformed into the same image from one degree of glory to another" (emphasis added). We don't "see" Christ literally and physically, of course (1 Peter 1:8). But His glory is on full display in the Word of God, and it is every minister's duty to make that glory known above all other subjects.

As believers gaze at the glory of their Lord—looking clearly, enduringly, and deeply into the majesty of His person and work—true sanctification takes place as the Holy Spirit takes that believer whose heart is fixed on Christ and elevates him from one level of glory to the next. This is the ever-increasing reality of progressive sanctification; it happens not because believers wish it or want it or work for it in their own energy, but because the glory of Christ captures their hearts and minds. We are transformed by that glory and we begin to reflect it more and more brightly the more clearly we see it. That's why the true heart and soul of every pastor's duty is pointing the flock to Christ, the Great Shepherd.

After more than four decades of pastoral ministry, I am still constantly amazed at the power of Christ-centered preaching. It's the reason I love preaching in the gospels. But I discovered long ago that the glory of Christ dominates Romans, Galatians, Colossians, Hebrews, Revelation—and the rest of Scripture as well. Focusing on that theme has led my own soul and our congregation to a fuller, richer knowledge of Christ—loving Him, worshipping Him, serving Him and yearning for the day when we shall be like Him, having seen Him in His glory (1 John 3:2).

Our prayer is that of Paul: "that I may know Him!" (Philippians 3:10). The apostle knew Him well as Savior and Lord (having been privileged to be the last person ever to see the resurrected Christ face to face, according to 1 Corinthians 15:8)—but never could Paul plumb the rich, sweet depths of the glories of Christ, the inexhaustible, infinite Treasure.

Far from allowing Christ to be eclipsed—even partially—by any other object or affection, every believer should pursue with relentless zeal the "full knowledge of the glory of God" provided by a fervent concentration "on the face of Christ" (2 Corinthians 4:6).

The Christian life *is* Christ—knowing Him in the height and breadth of His revelation, loving Him for the greatness of His grace, obeying Him for the blessing of His promises, worshipping Him for the majesty of His glory, and preaching Him for the honor of His Name: "But grow in the grace and knowledge of our Lord and Savior Jesus Christ. To Him be the glory both now and to the day of eternity. Amen" (2 Peter 3:18).

No greater subject exists than Jesus Christ—no greater gift can be given than uplifting His glory for another soul to see it and be changed by it. This book will be a wonderful help to anyone who senses the need to orient one's life and message properly with a Christ-centered focus. It is full of fresh, practical, and memorable spiritual insight that will show you how to remove whatever obstacle is blocking your vision of the Son and allow His light to blind you with joy.

—JOHN MACARTHUR

Pastor-Teacher, Grace Community Church, Sun Valley, California

April, 2011

Acknowledgments

Writing *Uneclipsing the Son* involved a year of conversations with people who sharpened and clarified my thinking about the comprehensiveness and exclusivity of Christ's supremacy in all things. What you are holding is the fruit of those interactions and the product of those friendships.

In the summer of 2010 I preached a sermon series to the college and singles ministry at Grace Community Church with the same title as this book. I want to thank those "Crossroaders" for their faithful listening and feedback. I approached my friend and publisher Rick Kress about the feasibility of turning the series into book form. His enthusiasm and support for the project never wavered. I will always be thankful for the privilege of publishing with Kress Biblical Resources. I remember hearing an author say, "There is no such thing as a good author, just a good editor." That is unmistakably the case with this book. Brian Thomasson edited this book and worked as hard on it as I did. His commitment and passion for seeing this project through is the main reason this book happened. Only God and his wife Jennifer know the sacrifices he made to contribute. This volume is much better because of Brian's editorial skills and insights. Working with him stretched my character and deepened my theology. Patti Schott, my secretary, not only typed the hundreds of pages of sermon transcripts for this project, but she also did it on her own time while never missing a step in serving our office and me. Her servant's heart makes everyone around her better. I want to thank Lisa Ham and Jennifer Barrow who did the intricate task of copy editing, as well as Katherine Lloyd for typesetting. There is a group of men who gave me much needed critical and theological feedback during the sermon series and throughout the writing process. Jesse Johnson, Mark Zhakevich, Justin McKitterick, Andrew Gutierrez, John Martin, Mike Elliott, and Nathan Busenitz listened, read, and contributed much. Also Jonathan Niednagel loaned me his ears and attention over many barbeque sandwiches and on a few hunting trips as I was marinating on the issues in the book. I also want to thank my pastor, John MacArthur for the inestimable contribution he has made in my life and ministry. The fingerprints of his teaching in this book will be obvious to anyone who knows him. As this book went to press I was in transition from being an associate pastor at Grace Community Church in Los Angeles to being the senior pastor at Mission Road Bible Church in Kansas City, KS. The elders of both churches granted me much understanding and grace as deadlines kept chasing me.

Most importantly, I want to thank my family. Luke, John, and Mark made significant sacrifices while Dad was downstairs in the study. And most significantly, I need to acknowledge my precious wife Kim. She heard every sermon, read every word, and provided me with the most valuable insights for this work. In Proverbs 31 a wise man named Lemuel asked, "An excellent wife, who can find?" When I get the chance to meet him in heaven I look forward to telling him, "I did."

Finally, I want to thank my Lord and Savior and Friend, Jesus. He "disclosed Himself" to me (John 14:21) in this study and I will never be the same. Oh, for that day when He will be finally and totally uneclipsed to me as my faith becomes sight. "Worthy is the Lamb that was slain to receive power and riches and wisdom and might and honor and glory and blessing" (Revelation 5:12).

1

THE CONCLUSION

I distinctly remember my first-grade teacher, Mrs. Cunningham, ushering our class outside to see a full solar eclipse in progress. For a kid who grew up with space on the brain, a kid whose dad woke him up in the middle of the night to see Neil Armstrong walk on the moon because he knew how important it was to him, this was a pretty big deal. Something happening in outer space was interrupting my school day, affecting the planet I lived on.

Here's what I remember about it: it was weird.

It wasn't light out, at least not the way we're used to. But it wasn't dark either. What light there was didn't have the quality of dusk or dawn. Our little first-grade class was engulfed in a giant shadow that swallowed up every other shadow. Colors lost their vibrancy. Everything around was a contrastless variation of gray. Why? Because the only light that was working on our part of earth, the schoolyard of Woodmore Elementary School in Chattanooga, Tennessee, was the light coming from the aura, from the corona of the sun.

Now, if you've experienced an eclipse, you know it's a very eerie experience. You find yourself suddenly in a world of half-light, a world lit only by the leftovers of the sun. And in the long years since that day in the schoolyard, I have come to see a similar kind of gray, spare light, a pervasive and all-covering shadow all but completely obscuring the glory of Christ. I think this is the great enemy to all of us who believe. Laboring in dealings with my own soul, working on my own sanctification, trying to increase my own love for Christ and that of those to whom I minister, I know what it is like to feel for the light switch in a world of spiritual gloom.

Jesus, the Son of God, has been eclipsed, and we've made ourselves at home in this new normal.

As we set out together to see if this is so, take a moment to check your heart for warning signs:

You've been told a thousand times to read your Bible, but it sits on the nightstand with pages still stuck together.

You've been convicted a thousand times more when you've been told to pray, but you never quite find the time and place.

You have a stack of Christian books that have been recommended. You have started some of them but finished very few.

You've begun to read your Bible, only to bail when you get to the numbers in Numbers.

How many times have you pillowed your head with great intentions of getting up early to spend time with God, and how many times have you hit the snooze button?

You believe that the gospel of Jesus Christ is true, you understand the realities of heaven and hell, but when it comes to witnessing, you feel a whole lot more like the Cowardly Lion in *The Wizard of Oz* than Jim Elliot of missionary lore. *Do I really want to tell this person the gospel? Can I muster the courage to engage in a simple conversation with someone who I know is going to hell unless they hear the gospel?*

You know you should be giving money to the church, but you're convinced that once that bill is paid, you'll start giving. Once you get that something you've really wanted, then you'll be in a position to sacrifice.

You've spent hours in church, listened to countless sermons, compiled enough notes to sink a battleship. You've had enough good intentions to compete with Mother Teresa and enough failures to compete with Peter's denials and Thomas's doubts. You've even resorted to making deals with

God. Still, something is woefully missing. There is a shadow, a pall over your very, very "normal" Christian life.

ABUNDANT EVERYTHING BUT LIFE

Let's come at it from another angle. In John 10:10, Jesus says very simply, "I came that they may have life, and have it abundantly." That little word *abundantly* is *perissos*. It means "exceptionally," "better than expected." According to Jesus, He came to provide us with this kind of life, but have you experienced it? Has your life in the gospel, has the gospel in your life, made such a radical difference that it's...*exceptional?*

Can you look in the mirror and say truthfully that there is a rich quality to your life that is better than expected?

Wouldn't you expect that Christ could affect in us that most basic purpose of His coming? He is God, very God after all! But we cannot consider this dilemma for long without concluding that surely the fault is not with the Son, but with us who have allowed Him to be...eclipsed. When the moon eclipses the sun, it is a wonder to behold. When anything eclipses Jesus, it is an atrocity to eradicate.

Think about this. There's never been a time like ours. Never have there been more resources for believers in Christ. Books, new versions and editions of the Bible, conferences, MP3s, DVDs, cool and hip churches, contemporary Christian music and radio stations, worship albums, blogs, websites, Christian Internet networks, and some of the best preachers in history, but still a broad shadow lingers over so many. Abundant resources have not yielded abundant life.

In fact, in honest conversations I've had with many Christians, I've heard the same sad theme. They bashfully talk about a deep struggle living out their faith. They live with a strange assumption that other believers are getting along just fine, while they are quietly, in the shadows, battling troubling doubts and debilitating sin. They wonder how everybody else is doing so well when they can't seem to find the spiritual equilibrium to walk— much less run—the Christian race. But the thought of being exposed is so terrifying that they begin to play the part, learn the Christian jargon, attend a steady succession of church events, surround themselves with those they believe have the "Christian thing" down and hope it will somehow rub off on them. But...somehow it hasn't.

Sooner than later, they find themselves facing the ultimate question, the question that seems so imminently logical in such a state: *Am I really saved? I keep struggling and struggling and looking around and feeling like no one else is struggling like this. Am I the only person who has these struggles in my heart with sin, these struggles in my mind with doubts?* Lying in bed, wondering if God is thinking about judging them, wondering what God thinks of them, does not make for restful nights. They grow weary, restless to do something to fix themselves.

So they ask Jesus to forgive them. Again. Rededicate their life. Again.

Before long, their fear of hell eclipses their desire for heaven. And no matter how many prayers, no matter how many re-rededications, they cannot seem to quite emerge into the full light of the Son.

Always clambering for the next handhold of assurance, they find themselves slipping back into the shadows.

YOU ARE NOT ALONE

Perhaps you have lived that out. Perhaps you're there right now. The truth is, I found myself nodding affirmation when I heard those stories, as they could easily describe my experience at many times in my own life. I too have wrung my hands, wondering how everybody can be doing so well while I'm a colossal failure spiritually. *What's wrong with me? Why can't I get my act together? Why can't I find the ignition switch for my faith?* Well, if those are your feelings, let me encourage you: you are not alone. In fact you've merely joined the ranks of some of Christianity's best-tended and most-blessed generations.

In the middle of the first century, only two decades after the crucifixion and resurrection of the Son of God, a young toddler church in modern-day Turkey was just finding its feet. There had been a revival in Jerusalem under the preaching of Peter, and the gospel was spreading powerfully and rapidly all over the ancient near east. And Christian persecutor-turned-missionary Paul was traveling from city to city preaching the gospel, explaining the truth about Christ, writing epistles.

And despite the fact the Paul had an unction to go tell his countrymen, the Jews, about salvation, God had a different plan. He said, "I want you to go to the Gentile cities, the Gentile nations." So Paul ended up touring through Ephesus, where he planted a church and stayed as their pastor for three glorious years.

Can you imagine Paul as your pastor? "Hey, Pastor Paul…err…*apostle of Christ,* Pastor Paul…how are you?" Paul—whose face still glowed with the glory of Christ who had appeared to him personally on the way to Damascus, who by all accounts, had a direct line with God the Father, who had seen a vision of heaven, who had been given the authority to speak for Christ Himself—was *their* pastor!

Can you imagine counseling calls with Pastor Paul? In Acts 20 Luke tells us that he went from house to house discipling the Ephesian believers. Can you picture that? "Hey, what's for dinner tonight?"

"I don't know, but Paul's coming over to visit."

"Really?!"

I imagine Paul probably didn't get a chance to eat much. They must have cornered him with questions that only he could authoritatively answer.

"What about Old Testament and New Testament? How does the circumcision fit in?"

"What about Jews and Gentiles?"

"Tell us about that rapture again."

"What was heaven like, really?"

"What did Jesus look like, in heaven?"

Paul. Was. Their. Pastor.

What an unbelievable blessing that must have been, basking in the glow of God's apostle—His chosen vessel—preaching and teaching, igniting their hearts with words from God!

To no one's surprise, it couldn't last. After three years that must have flown by, Paul was moved to continue his missionary efforts. He left Timothy, his son in the faith, to be the pastor there at Ephesus in his stead. Now, it's hard to imagine a better church situation: Paul for three years, and now you have Pastor Timothy! Ephesus was no doubt the megachurch of its day. Small groups were probably great, discipleship was happening, the preaching—are you kidding?—Paul and Timothy! They no doubt had the prototypical missions program, and you know the youth ministry was stellar. They even had a letter written to them that would end up in the Bible. It seems almost impossible to think that these believers would struggle in the way that you and I struggle, doesn't it?

But fast-forward thirty years—Paul and Timothy have both been martyred, and the apostle John was on the isle of Patmos, exiled. Instead of putting him in prison, the authorities put him out on an island, where Jesus came to him in a vision. While perhaps living in a cave, Christ appeared to John in blazing glory and had him take some divine dictation, writing letters to distribute to seven churches in Asia Minor. And the first church on that list to be sent a letter was the church at Ephesus. Not only did they get a letter written to them in the Bible, they got a second letter *from Jesus* recorded in the Bible.

But this letter had some teeth to it—it wasn't only praises. While Jesus acknowledged them for having a great deal of spiritual activity, saying in essence, "You guys have been busy; you've been doing a lot for Me," and praising them for standing for the truth, we find out that the unimaginable had happened to these mind-blowingly privileged Ephesian believers: *they had lost their love for Jesus.* With just a few words from His soul-piercing tongue, Jesus exposed them as deeply struggling Christians, not unlike you and me.

IT HAPPENED TO *THEM*

At this point, you may be wondering, *Why the history lesson?* Simply put, as we piece together the time line of what happened to the Ephesian

Christians, it's like watching the time-lapse images of an eclipse in progress.

One minute the Son is blazing; the next He is obscured; the next they are stumbling in half-light.

The story reaches back to Acts chapter 20, where Paul is making his way down the coast of Asia Minor on his way to Jerusalem. He's going to deliver an offering from the Macedonians to the Jewish believers in Jerusalem because those who had become believers had lost their jobs, lost their social standing, lost their position in the synagogue. They were literally starving to death and destitute. So the Macedonian believers up north had collected an offering to send down to the believers in Jerusalem so they could live, so they could carry on (see 2 Corinthians 8–9). Paul takes this generous gift and travels toward Jerusalem. Along the way, he stops and meets with the Ephesian elders.

Here's where the story takes a twist that makes the hairs on the back of your neck stand up. When Paul talks to those elders who had traveled over thirty miles to the coast to meet with him at Miletus, his words to them pack a wallop. He says, in essence, "This is the last time you men are going to see me. The Lord has informed me that I will be persecuted, imprisoned, and martyred." With the gravity of a deathbed exhortation, he tells them, "There's something else I need to tell you that's going to be very, very critical for the future of your church."

"What is it, Paul?" You can imagine these elders, entrusted with the care of this influential and thriving church, hanging on every word.

"From among yourselves will arise wolves." They may well have expected Paul to warn them about any number of threats to the church from the outside—Nero, Rome, government officials. But no, Paul says with utmost solemnity that the greatest threat is going to come from *within.*

How in the world could that happen? The saints had been treated to the finest and richest teaching imaginable. They had the best theology; they had the apostle Paul; they had Timothy in their homes, discipling them and praying for them. How in the world could these leaders slip? How in the world could such a church slip?

Well, Jesus' answer to that unsettling conundrum is in the very words He dictated to them through the apostle John in Revelation 2: "But I have *this* against you, that you have left your first love" (v. 4).

The answer was not *what* was missing.

The answer was *Who*.

Unbelievably, Jesus had something against them: they had lost their first love. He was to be their first love—at the center of their affections—but their hearts had drifted. They had been very active in Christian things, very active in their church, very active in their community. But they had abundance, not abundant life—and somewhere in the clutter, they had lost their passion for Jesus.

These believers began in the broad daylight of the glory of Christ, but now they had managed to elbow Him into the shadows, into the periphery of their lives. Instead of being the point of their lives, He was only a part of their lives. They found themselves stumbling in that eerie almost-day. And now, from glory, the Glorious One indicts them and calls them back into His light.

It happened to them. It happened to *them*.

Why couldn't it then happen to you? Has it happened to you? Are you living in the otherworldly odd light of the eclipse? Straining to see, longing to experience that marvelous-sounding and seemingly unreachable abundant life Jesus came to deliver? As strange and unthinkable as it may seem, in the hurricane of Christian activity and the avalanche of "Christian things" in which most of us live, Jesus *Himself* can come up missing. Look around. Listen. Check your own heart. It's way too easy to begin to think of Christianity as behavior modification, as a limitation on what you can enjoy or maybe making a moral or political stand or a social alternative to the world. And when we slip unwittingly into this mind-set, we effectively estrange ourselves from Christ, which sets us on a hunt for satisfaction in the world. And when the world fails to satisfy our souls—and it will—we try harder to do better to fit in more with Christians and to feel better about ourselves. When this happens, we have entered the cycle that sends us spiraling into yet deeper frustration.

What's wrong with me?

I'll tell you—you've ceased to worship Jesus. After all, Christianity is the worship of Jesus Christ. It's the worship of Jesus Christ exclusively, and it's the worship of Jesus Christ comprehensively. He alone is worthy; He alone is God; He alone is the infinite sacrifice made for the sins of those who would believe. But it's comprehensive as well, which means that every part of our being should be engaged in the worship and honor of Jesus. If Jesus is who the Bible says He is, if He did what the Bible says He did, He is worthy of absolute, complete, exclusive, comprehensive attention and focus in our life. That's the conclusion of this book. That's the first and last word on the subject at hand. Worship this Jesus. Don't let Jesus be crowded out.

In 2 Corinthians 11:3, Paul expresses precisely my deep concern as I begin this book. He says, "But I am afraid that, as the serpent deceived Eve by his craftiness, your minds will be led astray from the simplicity and purity of devotion to Christ." Something simple and pure is before us: the worship of Jesus Christ. Paul, a man who proclaimed the gospel in hostile synagogues and in open Gentile marketplaces, debated on the Areopagus of Athens, and evangelized the very council at Jerusalem who had murdered Jesus. Paul, who was beaten so badly at Lystra that he was left for dead, who stood for the gospel before Agrippa and Felix and before Roman guards holding him at sword point while in jail. Paul, who in Acts 17 is called one who "upset the world," is *afraid*. Fearless Paul is afraid that we will cease to simply and purely worship Jesus.

The truth is, there is nothing more terrifying than to miss Jesus, to be so close to Christian things but find yourself aloof from Christ and living in the half-light. God forbid that any of those He calls His own should linger in the shadows, in the backwaters of confusion and disillusionment. This has always been Satan's plan.

GETTING JESUS RIGHT

Before we get too far, I want to challenge you to get Jesus right. Robert M. Bowman and J. Ed Komoszewski provide these helpful words: "In our quest to know who Jesus was and is, we must give careful attention to the under-standing of Jesus presented in the sources closest to him: the New Testament Writings."[1] The entirety of the New Testament is devoted to getting Jesus right. These biblical books are not a mere directive for a new way to live, but a manifesto of the amazing greatness of Jesus. Get Jesus wrong and you lose everything that matters; get Him right and you gain everything that matters.

Let me supply a simple catalog to make sure from the outset that we're talking about the same Jesus. I encourage you to work through this list of who Jesus is with an open Bible and a prayerful spirit.

1. Jesus is revealed by and known through Scripture.

   - In Matthew, we meet Jesus as the fulfillment of the prophecies and longings of the Old Testament. Our Lord walks through Matthew's gospel wearing the banner of Jewish Messiah.

   - Mark provides a rapid-paced panorama of Jesus' march to the cross. The Savior is painted as the suffering Servant in these short sixteen chapters.

   - Luke was tasked by the Holy Spirit to show that Jesus was not only the Messiah for the Jews; He was also the only Savior for the whole world. The only Gentile writer in the New Testament, Luke writes of Jesus, in his Gospel and in the book of Acts, as the great missionary God, who desires to see all men come to know His only begotten Son as Lord and Savior.

   - Then there is John. He was the disciple Jesus loved. They shared a special relationship. Perhaps Jesus' best friend, John was inspired by the Spirit to write twenty-one chap-ters that present and interpret Jesus as the God-man, the Word made flesh.

   - Next we have the epistles (the letters of the New Testa-ment). Thirteen of these epistles were written by the apostle Paul. In Romans and Galatians, he explained the divine logic and theology behind God justifying sinners through Jesus' life and death.

- In 1 and 2 Thessalonians, Paul shows Jesus as heaven's Judge who is coming to adjudicate the world.
- In 1 and 2 Corinthians, he reveals Christ's intimate concern for and involvement in every dimension of His church.
- Writing from prison, Paul instructed the Ephesians, Colossians, Philippians, and Philemon that Jesus' rule and lordship extends to every part of the believer's life.
- The half brother of Jesus, James, wrote of Jesus as the rule and standard of all spiritual instruction.
- The anonymous writer to the Hebrews provided a hinge between the Old Testament and the new covenant by showing that Jesus is not only the Great High Priest but also, at the same time, the once-for-all sacrifice for sin.
- It was given to Peter to encourage suffering saints with the hope and power of Jesus who suffered unjustly, leaving us an example to emulate.
- Jude wrote a twenty-five-verse apologetic that all truth and error are defined by the Person of Jesus.
- Finally, in three little letters, John wrote of Jesus as the criterion and source of assurance of salvation. And the Spirit of God gave to Jesus' precious earthly friend a vision of His great and coming revelation at the end of all things in the book of Revelation.

2. Jesus is the one true God (Matthew 1:23; 2 Corinthians 4:4–6; Colossians 2:9; 1 Timothy 3:16; 6:15; Titus 2:13; Hebrews 1:2–3, 8; 1 John 5:20).

3. Jesus is a real man (1 Timothy 2:5; Hebrews 2:9–18; 4:14–16; 1 John 4:2).

4. Jesus is risen from the dead (Luke 12:31–34; Acts 2:24, 31; 4:2, 33; 5:30; 10:40; 13:30; 17:3; 1 Corinthians 15:12–19; Hebrews 13:20).

5. Jesus is the only way to God (John 3:16; 14:6; Acts 4:12; Hebrews 7:25; 1 Corinthians 15:3–4; 1 Peter 3:18; 1 John 2:2).

6. Jesus is the returning King (John 14:2–3; Acts 1:9–11; Revelation 19:11–16).

7. Jesus is Lord (John 13:13; Acts 5:31; 13:23; Romans 10:9; 14:9; Philippians 2:5–11; in the book of Acts, Jesus is referred to as Lord over ninety times, only twice as Savior).

HERE WE GO

I begin this book with fearful anticipation. A holy dread makes my fingers pause at the keyboard. I am not so arrogant as to think that the book you are holding is the answer to all your questions and the cure for all your soul's ills. But I am convinced that Jesus *Himself* is that Answer and Cure. I have experienced dry times in my faith and tried everything I could to quench my heart's thirst. But nothing has made a lasting difference, except Jesus.

My three sons and I love to fish. Recently, we came home from a decent day at the lake, and my hands were filthy (fishing is a messy business). In order to get all the dirt, worm slime, and fish guts off my hands, I removed my wedding ring. I set it on the coffee table and washed my hands. When I came back, I was panicked to see my dog, Daisy, sniffing the ring. However, she got a good sniff and walked away.

She had no idea the ring was made of valuable gold. She was clueless that it represented the promise I made to my wife. She was oblivious to how important that little metal circle is to me.

It *is* possible to see something and not grasp its worth. The pages that follow are my finite attempt to expose you to the infinite worth of Jesus. I am confident that if you will focus the eyes of your faith on the value of the Savior, you will emerge from the doldrums of the eclipse and enjoy the glory of the Son.

2

AMAZING LOVE, HOW CAN IT BE?

In case you were wondering, the sun has no surface.

It is a ball of perpetually exploding gas surrounded by an outer atmosphere called the corona, which is only about one-millionth as bright as the photosphere, the blazing core and fountainhead of all the heat and light in our solar system.

The sun's corona, also known as the aura, is what is visible during a solar eclipse. It's that ring of light around the silhouetted moon. The corona is only a kind of sideshow to the photosphere. When the moon comes into a position between our planet and the sun, it effectively blocks the photosphere and —temporarily, at least—draws our attention to that curious ring of light, which is *so* not the sun.

If you think about it, though, an eclipse is only strange to those who have stood in broad daylight. That sickly, faint half-light only seems so because we are accustomed to the light of the full sun on our world. We have watched it burn through thick fog and cause the morning dew to slip away from the grass in wisps of steam. We have watched its brilliant and glorious light spread indescribably beautiful spectra of color over the clouds, the landscape, and the sea, even as it sets. We know the sun because we wake to its light and walk in it all our days, but oddly, we rarely think about it unless its service is interrupted.

I hope you see where I'm going with this. As we began to explore in the first chapter, there is a real danger—one that made the apostle Paul tremble—of not knowing you're living in an eclipse because you have never truly walked in the warm and pure and all-satisfying light of Christ. There is a grave danger of mistaking the shadowland of the eclipsed Son of God for the broad daylight that the redeemed were redeemed to enjoy, thinking all along that this treadmill of Christian engagements, polite Christian conversations, and good Christian behavior is the abundant life Jesus came to earth to deliver and declare.

It isn't.

And perhaps nothing is more helpful in discovering this than asking yourself the question that Paul's magnum opus on the salvation Christ, the book of Romans, exists to answer:

What's the big deal? What's so great about the gospel?

It's a question that meets us right where we are in our lingering spiritual malaise. Do you know in your deepest being that the gospel is great and why? In Romans chapter 5, beginning in verse 6, the apostle Paul says this:

> For while we were still helpless, at the right time Christ died for the ungodly. For one will hardly die for a righteous man; though perhaps for the good man someone would dare even to die. But God demonstrates His own love toward us, in that while we were yet sinners, Christ died for us. Much more then, having now been justified by His blood, we shall be saved from the wrath of God through Him. For if while we were enemies we were reconciled to God through the death of His Son, much more, having been reconciled, we shall be saved by His life. And not only this, but we also exult in God through our Lord Jesus Christ, through whom we have now received the reconciliation. (vv. 6–11)

If you were to invite a person to church, a person who had never heard of Jesus, a person who had never read a Bible, a person who had never been in a worship service, a person who, say, knew only that there was a God and had a certain level of curiosity about Him, it would no doubt be an interesting experience to sit and watch his reaction to those words. Imagine for a moment that person standing next to you, hearing afresh, with curiosity even, words you have long ago filed away in your heart under Basic/Christian/Truth.

Distracted as he may be by his foreign surroundings, he hears...

We were helpless...Christ died.

While yet sinners...Christ died for us.

For the ungodly...God demonstrates love...for us.

Justified by...His blood.

Saved from the wrath of God...saved by His life.

We exult in God...through our Lord.

What is this about? The God I came to learn about, the Christ you told me I would hear about, died for the helpless, the ungodly? Think of the mystery, think of the audacity, the oddity, the incongruity, but most of all think of the nature, the flavor of the love described in those simple, strange, otherworldly words. It's not like any love your friend has heard of.

We hear these words with such familiarity that we don't realize the awesome weight of the statement they form. Living on the planet of this truth, we take the gravity of it for granted. Breathing the air of these ideas all our Christian days, we take our very life-sustaining atmosphere for granted.

Your friend's mind would be spinning, having just heard sets of words that are at once countercultural, nonintuitive, illogical, supernatural, mystical, and traumatizing. And in fact, unless the Lord was working in his heart, he might come away thinking that the "gospel," as you refer to it, is downright offensive.

But what's going on in *your* mind? What are you thinking? Do these words move you as they once did?

THE PROBLEM WITH ENFIELD

"Sinners in the Hands of an Angry God" is a sermon you probably heard about in high school. Few, though, understand the full context of Jonathan Edwards's famous homily. The leader in the most dramatic revival since Pentecost, one of history's greatest thinkers, and perhaps the most important of all American philosophers and theologians, Edwards was also an endearing husband, loving father to eleven children, piercing preacher, tireless mentor, compassionate missionary, and even a university president. In 1741, in New England, he was called upon to visit the holdout city of the Great Awakening, the city of Enfield, Connecticut. While entire cities were turning to Christ en masse, Enfield wanted nothing to do with Him.

One of the pastors in that area called the people "thoughtless and vain, and hardly conducting themselves with common decency."[1] Edwards was invited to preach a series, along with some other preachers, to try to wake up Enfield to the realities of heaven and hell. They got together in the cities that surrounded the districts of Enfield and set up a calendar of preaching events and set about to awaken them to gospel truths.

George Marsden writes about the experience, "Edwards could take for granted...that the New England audience knew well [the] gospel remedy. The problem was to get them to seek it."[2] Getting these gospel naysayers to stay awake, much less seek the truth, was no easy task. On July 8, 1741, a Wednesday evening, Edwards took the pulpit and began to preach. The sermon should have taken about forty-five minutes but went on much longer, because as the intensity of the sermon built, he had to stop several times and ask for silence so he could be heard.

Stephen Williams was there and recorded what happened. Williams writes, "Before the sermon was done, there was such a great moaning and crying throughout the whole church building. People were screaming, 'What shall I do to be saved?!' 'Oh, I'm going to hell!' 'What shall I do for Christ?!'"[3] Why? Because the sermon was exactly about the title, sinners in the hands of a God who was very, very angry. Edwards's point was very

16

simple—life is full of deadly uncertainties, and God is rightly angry with those who haven't received His Son in salvation.

And Edwards didn't spare the Enfielders any details. The sermon was loaded with some of the most graphic imagery in the English language to describe the sinful, horrific condition of an unconverted soul. Perhaps you're familiar with this very famous paragraph:

> The God that holds you over the pit of hell, much as one holds a spider, or some loathsome insect over the fire, abhors you, and is dreadfully provoked: His wrath towards you burns like fire; He looks upon you as worthy of nothing else, but to be cast into the fire; He is of purer eyes than to bear to have you in His sight; you are ten thousand times more abominable in His eyes, than the most hateful venomous serpent is in ours. You have offended Him infinitely more than ever a stubborn rebel did his prince; and yet it is nothing but His own hand that holds you from falling into the fire every moment. It is to be ascribed to nothing else, that you did not go to hell last night except for His grace; that you were permitted to awake again in this world, after you closed your eyes to sleep. And there is no other reason to be given, why you have not dropped into hell since you arose in the morning, but that God's hand has held you up. There is no other reason to be given why you have not gone to hell, since you have sat here in the house of God, provoking His pure eyes by your sinful wicked manner of attending his solemn worship. Yea, there is nothing else that is to be given as a reason why you do not at this very moment drop down into hell. O sinner! Consider the fearful danger you are in.[4]

It's difficult to imagine a pastor going to candidate at a church and starting with that sermon, but Edwards knew that the people would never seek the remedy unless they understood the grave illness with which they were afflicted. He knew the greatness of the gospel would not be seen until the eclipse of sinful sluggishness diminished and they could picture in their minds the precariousness of their state.

You see, the problem with Enfield may be our problem as well. Surrounded by converts, we've ceased to be convinced that our illness is all that grave, that the thread from which we are suspended is all that thin. And so, as with the Enfielders, we cannot for the life of us remember what's so great about the gospel. We need someone faithful to stir us up again, to point us back to that first love. We need to be moved and to be reawakened.

THE GREATNESS OF THE GOSPEL

In Romans 5 language, this means we need to understand afresh what words like *helpless, ungodly,* and *sinner* mean so that we can feel the way words like *Christ died for us* are meant to make us feel. When the judgment that awaits us is personal, we long for a salvation that is personal and real and effective at every level. That's where Paul takes us in Romans 5. He defines the precious doctrine of justification, how you can be made right in the eyes of this God who does indeed abhor us like some loathsome creature held over a fire. How can we be reconciled to Him?

The answer to that question is the greatness of the gospel, and the gospel is the only way to remove any and every obstacle obscuring the blazing glory of Jesus Christ. It's our only hope for living in His fullness. The gospel is the only leverage powerful enough to roll away the stone from our hearts. Without a great gospel, you are forever in the shadow world of eclipse, of despondency, of hypocrisy.

THE BLACK BACKDROP

Paul sets up his description of the gospel's inherent greatness by laying down the backdrop, the black backdrop of human sin. Only when we understand how wicked we truly are—how desperate our condition is, how hopeless and helpless our plight—will we know to reach for the gospel remedy. We will never understand the greatness of the gospel if we do not pause to consider the greatness of the need it was designed to satisfy.

Paul says in verse 6, "For while we were still helpless, at the right time Christ died for the ungodly." Few, it seems, have taken the time for such a consideration. One church's website records this testimony of a new believer: "Here, I have found pastors who teach gently in the way of Christ…absent of judgment, without condemnation, good people to share the best of what means the most to them."

As pleasant as the words sound, we might ask ourselves, *Is that biblical Christianity, "a friendly place for personal sharing"*? If there is no judgment, no condemnation, what need does the gospel meet for such a congregation? If God is not angry, what need have we of Christ to appease Him personally, with His own blood? The worst of possibilities and realities are not put out of mind in the Christian gospel; they're held central in the foolishness of God to crucify His Son for those under His rightful judgment and condemnation.

Paul belabors his description of these realities, lest we miss them. In verse 6 he says that we're "helpless," and then that we're "ungodly." In verse 8 he calls us simply "sinners." And in verse 10 he says that we're "enemies" of God. Helpless, ungodly sinners who are enemies of God—that's our biography; that's our spiritual pedigree. What does all that mean?

A helpless person is unable to understand spiritual things, according to 1 Corinthians 2:14.

He is unable to see the kingdom of God or enter into it, according to John 3:3 and John 5.

He is unable to seek God, according to Romans 3:11.

And helplessness is nowhere better summed up than in Ephesians 2:1, where Paul says simply that we are "dead in [our] trespasses and sins."

To be helpless is to be a blind man in an art gallery, a deaf man at a symphony. It's like trying to pick up an FM signal with an AM radio… without a battery…with a broken antenna…and every wire inside has been cut…the knobs have been broken off…the guts of the radio have been extracted…there's no on/off switch…you have no hands on your body to even touch it…and the radio is on the moon.

And one more thing. You're dead.

That's the picture of helplessness. You can't do anything to even *begin* to secure the remedy you so profoundly require. But beyond this, Paul explains in verse 6 that we were "ungodly," our very nature in fierce opposition to God—in conscience and in morals. Romans 1:18 says, "For the wrath of God is revealed from heaven against all ungodliness and unrighteousness of men who suppress the truth in unrighteousness." We are those who ourselves eclipse the truth in unrighteousness, effectively blocking off our only hope.

So there we are. Anti-God and dead to Him.

Hopeless.

But then, "at the right time," the apostle explains, "Christ died for [us]." At the right time in the progression of human history, at the determined hour in prophetic revelation, and at the darkest but most perfect time in reference to our sin-wrecked souls, Christ died…for us. Bound by sin and advancing toward an eternity apart from God in hell, no amount of struggle could ever free us from such condemnation, yet the cross happened at the divinely appointed time.

All of history marched toward the cross, before that afternoon on Calvary, and everything has flowed from it since. The crucifixion of Jesus Christ on the hill outside of the temple mount gate is the central event in all of human history. Christ died as our representative, in our place. How unlikely! How completely mismatched were we with this One who paid our ransom!

This is the great doctrine of substitution, the great doctrine of propitiation, God taking out His wrath on Someone in our place. Our greatest need is not defined by the gurus of modern psychology: Skinner, Freud, Pavlov, or Rogers. Our greatest need is not defined by the Home Shopping Network, nor is it found on glossy catalog pages. Our greatest need is the debt we owe God because of our sin. You need a substitute—a perfect and willing Savior.

Do you understand and feel the greatness of the gospel as you see it suited to your greatest need?

AMAZING LOVE, HOW CAN IT BE?

As Paul paints the greatness of the gospel, he does not leave unanswered the question of why Christ died and why God would have Him do so. If he had, we might be left to imagine a sterile cosmic transaction of some kind. But because our offense against God was personal and because the state that offense left us in was so totally helpless, God had to act unilaterally to redeem us, and He had to find the will to do so within Himself.

What was it that compelled Him?

Love.

Love for *us*?

As difficult as it is to imagine, God acted out of love for us. Yes, *us*. Paul elaborates for us in our total bewilderment at this unimaginable love. He gives an illustration in verse 7: "For one will hardly die for a righteous man; though perhaps for the good man, someone would dare even to die." The character in Paul's story is described as "good" and "righteous"; he's a good guy, respectable. Someone might die for a guy like that.

Such a person would appeal to the affections of another, perhaps soliciting the ultimate sacrifice. We have all heard stories of a grenade being thrown into a location with several soldiers and one of them instinctively and instantly diving on it, absorbing the blast and saving his friends. That kind of noble, sacrificial action makes good sense to us.

Stories like that define what it means in our minds to love. But God's definition of His own love is taken from an entirely different dictionary, which derives its definitions from His own ineffable character. There is a vast gulf of difference between God's love and even the loftiest ideals of human love, as Paul goes on to explain: "But God demonstrates His own love toward us, in that while we were yet sinners, Christ died for us."

Paul asks us to stand back and consider a demonstration—a permanent cosmic display—of God's kind of love. God doesn't dive on the grenade, dying for His friends. Christ dies, instead, for His enemies: ungodly, unrighteous, helpless people. Spurgeon wrote, "God hath manifested His love in the death of Christ in a way which must have astonished every inhabitant of heaven, and it ought to ravish every native of this lower globe."[5]

How can we not be astonished at this?

In 1 Peter 1:12, Peter says that angels long to look into the things of salvation. And sometimes I like to imagine that moment when,

after the trials,

after the beatings,

after the scourging,

looking down from heaven, all of the angelic hosts are watching Jesus, God in the flesh, walking through the holy city of Jerusalem, carrying a cross, hanging on a tree to die. I picture every angel with his toes curled over the edge of heaven and his sword drawn saying, "Let me go, Father. I'll defend Your Son."

But the Father says nothing, does nothing. Jesus cries out, "Why have You forsaken Me?"

No answer.

Jesus pleads, "Take this cup from Me."

No answer.

If the angels look into the mystery of salvation and are baffled and awestruck, how much more should we? The angels watched God decisively judge so many of their kind at the beginning for their rebellion. Now they see this God extend His judgment to His own Son so that He might deluge generations of rebels with mercy and grace and total forgiveness. It's inconceivable, but it's real.

My favorite hymn is Charles Wesley's "And Can It Be?" Read through all the verses of this classic sometime and take note of how personal it is. The entire hymn is an overwhelmed reflection on God's love. I believe that the chorus might be some of the best words ever penned.

Amazing love! How can it be
That Thou, my God, should die for me?

Imagine the thoughts of that visitor you brought to church when these lyrics show up on the screen. Jesus, fully God and truly man, died *for me*? Hopeless, helpless, sinful enemies of God—we too should sing about such amazing love. We too should ask, "How can it be?"

In the cross we see a constant, ongoing object lesson of God's love— "His own love," as Paul describes it (v. 8). No one loves likes God does. The cross is the most amazing event to ever occur, the most amazing thought to ever be conceived, and the question of your life is: Are you amazed? Do you see the greatness of the gospel as you weigh the quality and the contours of this love...*for you*?

SAVED—FROM GOD

In verse 9 of Romans 5, Paul opens the darkest, most fearful closet in Christian theology and turns on the light. He writes, "Much more then, having now been justified by His blood, we shall be saved from the wrath *of God* through Him." There is so much theology in this verse that we could spend the rest of the book exploring its truth.

Dominating its skyline is the wrath of God. We usually think of salvation as being saved from hell, and it is. We easily think of salvation as being saved from sin, and it is. We often think of salvation as being saved from self, and it is. However, Paul informs us here that salvation is being saved—from God. He is rightfully angry with us and at us (Romans 1:18–32). Our sin draws His wrath like a magnet draws steel.

God's wrath is an incredibly intimidating subject because it forces us to wrestle with the reality of hell. Many people consider hell little more than a manipulative superstition for scaring people into compliance. The Bible emphatically says otherwise.

Warning people of the wrath to come was at the center of Edwards's famous sermon. Put yourself for a moment in a dimly lit Enfield pew on that humid July evening. Mr. Edwards crescendos, "Unconverted men walk over the pit of hell on a rotten bridge, and there are innumerable places in this bridge so weak that they will not bear their weight, and these places are not seen. The arrows of death fly unseen at noon-day; the sharpest sight cannot discern them. God has so many different unsearchable ways of taking wicked men out of the world and sending them to hell, that there is nothing to make it appear, that God had need to be at the expense of a miracle, or go out of the ordinary course of his providence, to destroy any wicked man, at any moment."[6] Was Edwards trying to manipulate for some behavioral compliance, or was he faithfully warning these people of the wrath of God?

I think he was doing exactly what Paul was doing in Romans 5. The mention of God's wrath is a reference to the indefinable wonder that believers in Christ have been saved from God and His wrath. Verse 9 tells us we have been saved from His wrath through Jesus. How does this work? The text discloses the answer—through the blood of Jesus.

It might surprise you to know that very little blood was shed in a crucifixion. Death on a cross occurred because of asphyxiation, not blood loss. Sure, there was blood that came from the wounds of our Lord's hands and feet; sure, there was blood streaming down His back from the scourging; and sure, there was blood dripping down Jesus' face from the piercing crown of thorns; but He didn't die from blood loss. So why does Paul talk about blood?

This is a reference to the blood of the Old Testament sacrificial system. These animal sacrifices involved a lot of blood. Being made right before God—the doctrine of justification—is free, but it is not cheap. The Levitical system shed the blood of an innocent animal, costing its life. But in the gospel, blood of infinitely more value was shed, and a life supremely precious was sacrificed.

The writer to the Hebrews contrasts the difference between these two sacrifices: "Every priest stands daily ministering and offering time after time the same sacrifices, which can never take away sins; but He [Jesus], having offered one sacrifice for sins for all time, SAT DOWN AT THE RIGHT HAND OF GOD" (Hebrews 10:11–12). Jesus' death— *once for all*—paid the penalty for sin.

"IT'S GOOD NOT TO BE IN TROUBLE WITH GOD"

A few years ago, I was having a discussion with my son about the gospel. This particular conversation occurred after I had to correct something in his behavior. Trying to bring the exchange back to gospel truth, I tried to explain to him the fact that Jesus received the consequences of our disobedience to God on the cross. Now we can be sons to and friends with God. I will never forget his response. "Dad, it's so good not to be in trouble with God because of Jesus."

That's great theology. And that is exactly the point Paul makes in verse 10: "For if while we were enemies we were reconciled to God through the death of His Son, much more, having been reconciled, we shall be saved by His life." The gospel mediates the great conflict between God and sinners.

If God reconciled us as His enemies, surely He will save us in the end as His friends. This is a great verse for assurance. If you believe that God is powerful enough to save you through the gospel, why continue to worry about what happens when you die? Why lie in bed at night after a particularly bad day and wonder if you're truly saved?

Paul uses an argument from the greater to the lesser. Can you ever out-sin God's grace? How strong is your understanding of grace? Can you sing, "Grace that is greater than *all* my sin," or could you more easily sing, "Grace that is greater than the sin I feel bad about and have repented of"? Is His grace greater than all your sin or just certain sins? If God reconciled us through giving us His Son to die, He's going to reconcile us as His friends and save us from His wrath and put us in eternity with Him.

HOW EXCITED ARE YOU?

After five verses of explaining the treasures of the gospel, Paul erupts into an epic ovation to the Son of God: "And not only this, but we also exult in God through our Lord Jesus Christ, through whom we have now received the reconciliation" (v. 11). This is the response the gospel should provoke in us as well. Paul begins by asking us to see beyond even how God saved us in the past and will bring us to heaven in the future. These things are wonderful, but we exult in something further.

Understand Paul does not use the word *exalt* here, though there is plenty of cause for exaltation. Instead, Paul has in mind "exulting," which means "to emotionally engage with joy." The word portrays an overwhelmed and overflowing response to "our Lord Jesus Christ." We go about our days like a person navigating a crowd with a full glass of water. Every time somebody bumps us, we overflow with our joy in Christ alone.

Sometimes this kind of exulting doesn't seem likely…

Greg was one of my best friends. We went to junior high, high school, and college together. We played baseball together, took chemistry together, and even got into some mischief together. But most importantly, we went to church together. I had few friends closer than Greg.

I assumed Greg was truly converted as I went off to seminary.

In my second year of seminary in Los Angeles, I flew home to be with my family for Christmas. Greg called me to have lunch. It was a meal I will never forget. He began to explain to me that he had been saved. This was a bit surprising to me since I'd never had reason to question his faith. But he was emphatic that something profound had recently happened.

I knew something was different when he reached across the table and grabbed my hand. Greg was a weight lifter so when I instinctively tried to pull back my hand, it wasn't happening; my friend was strong.

"I've been saved, Rick," he said with a volume that made me almost as uncomfortable as his holding my hand. "Listen to me. I've really been saved by Jesus." His passion could not be contained. Every head was turning to look at the commotion his enthusiasm was creating.

"Yeah, I know, Greg. We grew up together," I answered.

Relentlessly and passionately he spoke even louder, "Rick, I'm not going to hell. I have *really* been saved!"

Something was very different about my friend. As he continued to explain himself, I turned from being embarrassed to being humbled. The food came and he just sobbed into it. He told me of all his doubts and his worry and his years in the twilight of Jesus. He never touched his food. Yes, he had grown up in the church and been faithfully involved. But Greg was never truly regenerated. He had been acting like a Christian but had no love for Jesus Himself. Through his reading of John's Gospel, he realized the emptiness of his soul and Jesus became gloriously uneclipsed.

Exultation was the reflex of his soul, and now it was pouring out on me over lunch.

Not long after that, my friend Greg became engaged to a godly woman. Six days before their wedding, she was killed in a head-on automobile collision. A year later he married her best friend. Not long after they were married, he had a headache that would not go away. Tests would reveal that he had terminal brain cancer.

I went to visit Greg after he had brain surgery to try to remove the tumor. The conversation we had is one of my favorite memories. With his head bandaged and eyes swollen from the operation, he asked me if I thought God was in control of everything—including the cancer cells in his body. I swallowed hard and said yes.

Tears began to roll down his cheeks, and a smile curled from his lips. "If God is sovereign over my cancer, I can go through this," he said.

Then he began to tell me how excited, curious, and ready he was to see Jesus. For Greg, dying was gain (Philippians 1:21) because his faith would become sight (1 Corinthians 13:12; 2 Corinthians 4:6–9, 18).

As we end this chapter, ask yourself what you are overflowing with. Can you see through your circumstances to exult in Jesus? Do you have a faith that longs for sight? Has the gospel made you tremble lately? Has it made you weep for joy? Has it settled you with a deep and satisfying peace? Can you say with unabashed happiness, "It's good not to be in trouble with God"?

3

ETERNAL LIFE IS
NOT WHAT YOU THINK

Martians.

We roll our eyes at the thought of a martian, especially the sophisticated, saucer-flying, short-and green-with-an-antenna kind of martian. But there was a time when this wasn't just science fiction; it was actually considered good science. A generation ago widespread public opinion held that intelligent life did indeed exist on Mars. Books were written about martians, magazines speculated about their alien society, and Hollywood made a lot of money putting the theory on the big screen. But have you ever wondered where the idea originated? Who was it that started all this hullabaloo?

As it turns out, at the end of the nineteenth century an influential astronomer named Percival Lowell became convinced that there was intelligent life on Mars. He conducted extensive research on Mars using the most powerful telescope of the day. The result was a detailed map of the martian surface. This map revealed an elaborate matrix of canals that Lowell believed to be the lifelines of martian society.

He published his findings in 1906 in a book called *Mars and Its Canals*. Two years later he released a second book entitled *Mars As the Abode of Life*. Percival Lowell had become the leading scientific expert for life on Mars. Emboldened by his findings, Lowell speculated about the day when earthlings would meet these martians. He wrote, "Not only do the observations we have scanned lead us to the conclusion that Mars at this moment is inhabited, but they land us at the further one that those denizens [or "citizens"] are of an order whose acquaintance was worth the making. Whether we ever shall come to converse with them in any more instant way is a question upon which science at present has no data to decide."[1]

Lowell was right, as we all now know. One day science would indeed decide if we would ever have a conversation with the inhabitants of Mars.

The answer is no. Martians don't exist.

From the pictures taken of Mars by *Mariner 4* in 1965 and *Mariner 9* in 1972, Lowell's proof of a martian society evaporated in the heat of hard scientific data. Remember all those movies in the fifties about martians? They were based on his research. What was he talking about? Where did he get this alleged surface map of the red planet?

Of all the things people knew about Percival Lowell, nobody accused him of or thought him to be a fraudulent scientist trying to make a name for himself. Instead, experts have speculated that Lowell suffered from a rare eye disorder. When looking through the eyepiece of his telescope, his eye focused on the reflection on the back of his eyeball. He had no way of discerning the difference between the martian surface and the amazing array of vessels imposed on it by the trick of his eye.

That's right. He spent years mapping the blood vessels on the back of his eyeball, placing the weight of his reputation on this massive misunderstanding. And while science fiction writers and moviemakers of the fifties were all the better for it, it was hardly a giant leap for humankind scientifically speaking.

Let's take this to our understanding of the gospel and of the abundant life that Jesus Christ, the blazing Son of God, offers us in it. Even if we understand and know in our deepest being the greatness of the gospel, spiritually speaking that same eye disorder can affect any of us. If left to instinct, if left to intuition, if left to merely imitating the

Christians in proximity to us, an unavoidable projection occurs.

When we try to conceptualize what fellowship with this God looks like, when we try to think about what abundant life in Jesus really means, the natural tendency is to imagine that God is kind of like us. That He thinks likes us, sees things like us, that His ways are like ours instead of being so utterly and completely "other" than ours, as the writers of Scripture endlessly reiterate (Isaiah 55:8–9; Romans 11:33). When we try to look at divine things, we inevitably see a reflection of our own souls, as God Himself says so succinctly in Psalm 50:21: "You thought I was just like you."

Likewise, we imagine that a relationship with our Creator is no different qualitatively than any of our earthly relationships. We suppose that the worship of God is mechanistic—that we need only "perform it" rather than deeply and personally engage in it.

Why?

Perhaps we imagine that God is capricious and superficial, as we often are, that He longs to rate our performance rather than to know us and be known by us. Convinced of this, we begin to look at our walk with Him as an empty drudgery because we impose on His person the lie that Satan taught our first parents in the Garden: that He is not good, that He is not personable, that He cannot satisfy us.

YOUR SOUL DISORDER

Are you staking your eternity on a vague understanding of the nature and quality of what eternal life actually is or, what it's meant by God to be like, to feel like, to enjoy?

Are you caught up in the fray of Christian culture but secretly unsure of what all the excitement is about?

Are you going through your days with that wearying feeling of indefinable emptiness, like you've lost something incredibly important— essential even—but you can't remember what it is?

The condition of your soul is a mirror reflection of what you worship.

Internal struggles, emotional instability, upsetting doubts—these are really theological problems disguised as earthly troubles. Wrong thinking about Jesus and the salvation He offers will metastasize into a debilitating soul cancer. These disorders in our souls are directly related to our understanding, or misunderstanding, of eternal life.

THE BEST-KNOWN, LEAST-UNDERSTOOD LIFE

John 3:16.

It's held up at football games when people are kicking extra points and field goals; people strap it on themselves and run across the playing field. I was at an intersection the other day and a guy was standing there with a big sandwich board placard that said simply, "John 3:16." We love this verse…

> "For God so loved the world, that He gave His only begotten Son, that whoever believes in Him shall not perish, but have eternal life."

But what do we love about it? What promise does it contain that makes the verse so universally helpful?

God so loved the world that He gave His only Son. But why?

So you could have eternal life. But have you ever noticed that the verse does not describe what this eternal life actually is?

Now, defining eternal life seems simple. Just look at the two words. *Eternal* means forever. *Life* means to be alive and not dead. Put them together and you get "living forever." Is this the definition of eternal life? If you looked at just the bare vocabulary, that's what you would be left with. In our Christian understanding, the idea of eternal life has become a synonym for living forever in heaven. But remember, even those who do not believe the gospel will indeed live forever—but not in heaven (Matthew 25:46; Jude 1:7). So what is this eternal life that Jesus offers?

In John 17, the Lord Himself gives us a definition of eternal life.

Interestingly, it has nothing to do with time. At the end of the Last Supper, Jesus is about to go out and suffer in the Garden of Gethsemane. So He offers a prayer on behalf of His disciples, the church, and the world. Jesus prays aloud in the presence of the disciples: "This is eternal life, that they may know You, the only true God, and Jesus Christ whom You have sent" (v. 3).

Surprisingly little there about living forever and nothing, it seems, about heaven. Everyone is listening, and Jesus takes the opportunity to define eternal life. But strangely He defines it as…knowing.

Eternal life is knowing the one and only God. This is why He sent His only Son to the world He loved. But how can we know that we know this God? We can't see Him, touch Him, hear Him. Our God-given senses can't sense God, remarkably enough.

In the next breath, Jesus fleshes out His definition, quite literally. Knowing the only God is knowing "Jesus Christ whom You have sent." It seems a little awkward, the way He words it—and it is. In fact, this is the only place in the Bible where Jesus refers to Himself in the third person. That's how important it is.

Jesus Christ knew that down through the ages there would be every opportunity to pollute and dilute and "update" the definition, the understanding of which is the key to the blessedness of humankind; and so He saw to it that the inscripturated sign, prayed with all the passion of His perfect being, would forever point solely and simply to Jesus Christ. Canonized, crystallized in these words, is the real promise of all those ball game banners. What is eternal life? Knowing Jesus. Knowing God through knowing Jesus.

Knowing God by knowing Jesus *is* Christianity. Becoming a Christian is engaging in a lifetime pursuit of knowing Jesus. This is just what Paul describes in Philippians 3:7–8: "But whatever things were gain to me, those things I have counted as loss for the sake of Christ. More than that, I count all things to be loss in view of the surpassing value of knowing Christ Jesus my Lord." Everything in Paul's life is disposable except Jesus.

Paul's example and Jesus' definition shape, or really should *reshape*, the focus of our faith. A distinction must be made here, though, between *knowing about* Jesus and *knowing* Jesus. Whatever it means to know Christ, it has the most urgent and eternal ramifications. Pair Jesus' definition of eternal life with this warning He gave at the conclusion of the Sermon on the Mount:

"Not everyone who says to Me, 'Lord, Lord,' will enter into the kingdom of heaven; but he who does the will of My Father who is in heaven. Many will say to me on that day, 'Lord, Lord, didn't we prophesy in Your name, and in Your name cast out demons, and in Your name perform many miracles?' And then I will declare to them, 'I never knew you; DEPART FROM ME, YOU WHO PRACTICE LAWLESSNESS.'" (Matthew 7:21–23)

Do you notice how knowing is a two-way street? We know Jesus, we know God through Jesus, and Jesus knows us as well. Being God, Jesus knows about everything, but in this scene at the Great Judgment, only those He knows personally, salvifically enter into heaven. The great gospel, which we considered in the last chapter, has brought us to this hallowed place, but our own thin understanding of how to proceed in it may greatly limit our satisfaction in and thus our effectiveness for Christ. We go forward by knowing and being known by Jesus—Jesus Christ whom God has sent.

When God saves a person, He calls him into "fellowship with His Son, Jesus Christ our Lord" (1 Corinthians 1:9). Fellowship with our living Redeemer (Job 19:25) is one of the great sensations of faith. This fellowship is real, as real as a shared meal. Jesus said, "Behold, I stand at the door and knock; if anyone hears My voice and opens the door, I will come in to him and will dine with him, and he with Me" (Revelation 3:20). At the Last Supper, the Lord described His fellowship with believers as even more extensive than sharing a meal. It is actually more like having a permanent roommate: "If anyone loves Me, he will keep My

34

word; and My Father will love him, and We will come to him and make Our abode with him" (John 14:23).

Do you see the connection here? Jesus defined eternal life as knowing God the Father and Jesus Christ whom He sent (John 17:3; also see 1 John 1:1–4). And this spiritual relationship is possible because of the permanent, abiding presence of the Father and the Son with His children. What sweet, unspeakable grace there is in the fact that the glorious experience and enjoyments of heaven have not made our Savior indifferent to fellowship with us, His sin-stained and earthbound children. Have you experienced this fellowship? Are you aware of this divine presence? Do you seek to enjoy and honor and feel the fellowship of the risen, living Jesus?

What does that feel like? It's all about appraising Jesus as infinitely and personally precious. It is about a conscious, deliberate enjoyment of His worth.

MY PRECIOUS

J. R. R. Tolkien's epic Lord of the Rings trilogy contains some of the most unforgettable characters in English literature. At the head of the list is Gollum. This wretched, two-faced, pitiful creature poisoned with desire has one overarching characteristic. He's obsessed with the gold ring of power.

He extols the ring endlessly. He lies to get access to the ring. He even murdered his brother to obtain the ring. Throughout the series, Gollum's obsession is portrayed in how he describes, even talks to, this ring. He calls it "my Precious." The ring was so valuable to Gollum that he gave it a pet name. Tolkien, through Gollum, compressed all the value he could into this one simple word—*precious*.

The word *precious* describes something of high price or great value. What we deem as precious has the greatest effect on our lives. Gollum illustrates the dark side of this principle. Valuing the wrong thing will poison your soul and create a devil in the mirror. However, there is another kind of obsession that transforms the soul into the image of Christ. That obsession is Jesus Himself.

The apostle Peter had this obsession. It motivated his ministry. It dominated his decisions. It was worth a martyr's death. Gollum's precious was a ring to possess. Peter's precious was a Savior to worship.

In his first epistle, Peter provides a glorious insight into what was most precious to him and what is to be most precious to every believer. First Peter 2:7 is not the easiest verse to translate from the original Greek. Look at a few translations and you will quickly notice that there are differences of opinion about how to render Peter's words. It may seem a bit out of vogue, but I believe the *King James Version* actually makes the clearest sense in English of what Peter wrote in Greek. It reads, "Unto you therefore which believe he [Jesus] is precious." There it is. To those who believe, Jesus is precious. This precious value is the brilliance of the Son of God behind the eclipse.

When Jesus defined eternal life as knowing God through Himself, He placed the ultimate reality—living forever—in the dimension of relationship, not the space-time continuum. Eternal life is the uneclipsed appraisal of Jesus as the most precious reality. In verse 4, Peter tells us that Jesus is the Living Stone, rejected by men but precious and choice in the sight of God. When a believer values Jesus as precious, he is actually joining the Father's assessment of the Son. This appraisal will never disappoint the evaluator—"I LAY IN ZION A CHOICE STONE, A PRECIOUS CORNER *stone*, AND HE WHO BELIEVES IN HIM WILL NOT BE DISAPPOINTED" (v. 6). Sorry to sound like a city bus billboard, but…

Disappointed? Discouraged? Depressed? Jesus and Jesus alone must become the volume and the value of your life.

FROM DENIAL TO DELIGHT

How did Peter come to these conclusions? How did he figure out that eternal life is knowing and valuing Jesus?

Let's rewind the gospel record a few decades. Before Peter's spiritual maturity parked on Jesus' preciousness, he drove the sports car of his pride with reckless impulsiveness. Somewhere between Galilee and Jerusalem, Peter began to connect the dots. Follow along as I summarize the conversation he had with Jesus and the other eleven disciples (Matthew 16:13–23). The Lord says, "All right, let's talk about the rumors, guys. I know people are talking about Me. I'm feeding people; I'm healing people; I'm teaching people. What are they saying about Me? Who do they say I am?"

Some of the disciples answer, "Well, um, you know actually, Lord, it's interesting that You should ask because some people think that, um, I don't know how to tell you this but that, um, John the Baptist has been reincarnated in You. And if that's not weird enough, others think that you're a reincarnated prophet, like Elijah or Jeremiah."

Then Jesus says, "Who do *you* say that I am?"

Peter, boldly and loudly, rose to the challenge. He was not going to miss this opportunity. "You are the Christ, the Son of the Living God!"

And Jesus gives Peter the most significant affirmation of his life.

"You're right! Flesh and blood didn't tell you this. God did."

Peter must have been glowing. In fact, he was so filled with confidence that he pulled Jesus aside and gave the Savior some unsolicited counsel.

"Listen, Master, this whole thing about going to the cross? We need to rethink it. You're the Christ, the Son of the Living God. You're not going to any cross. Crosses are for criminals. You're not going to die!"

But as Peter, the disciple with the foot-shaped mouth, begins to think he might prevail on the Lord with his more practical approach, Jesus says to him, "Get behind me, *Satan!*"

Peter's confession about the Lord's identity was his Mount Everest in his relationship with Christ. A moment later, his altitude dropped to Dead Sea level.

And it got worse.

Not long afterward came the eve of Jesus' crucifixion. After the final supper, Jesus told them they were moments away from abandoning Him. Quoting Zechariah 13:7, He said, "You will all fall away because of Me this night, for it is written, 'I WILL STRIKE DOWN THE SHEPHERD, AND THE SHEEP OF THE FLOCK SHALL BE SCATTERED'" (Matthew 26:31).

Peter responded, "Even though all may fall away because of You, I will never fall away" (v. 33).

With divine foresight, Jesus replied, "Truly I say to you that this very night, before a rooster crows, you will deny Me three times" (v. 34).

Peter said to Him, "Even if I have to die with You, I will not deny You." All the disciples echoed this (v. 35).

You know the rest of the story. Peter denied that he was in any way associated with Jesus three times in the next few hours.

His love for Jesus had been eclipsed by his love for his own safety.

A few days after Jesus' resurrection, Peter returned north to Galilee and resumed his fishing job. He was working the shallows just offshore, close enough to hear a voice call to him from land. It was Jesus.

"How's the fishing?"

"Not good," Peter replied.

"Throw the net on the right side of the boat."

At the beck and call of the Creator, every tilapia in the area furiously finned its way into the net. The fastest ones made it in. So large was the catch that these professional anglers couldn't get the net into the boat.

Peter knew it was Jesus. Not wanting to take the necessary time to deal with the catch, he left the work to the other four and dove into the water, swimming as fast as possible to get to the shore.

I can almost see the embrace between these two friends when Peter made the shoreline. Tears, smiles, laughter, and heartful love that swallowed the deny-er's disbelief and shame. Jesus was back, and He had for Peter one question for every denial.

"Peter, do you love Me?"

"Peter, do you love Me?"

"Peter, do you love Me?"

Not, "Do you have your philosophy of ministry down?" Not, "Do you have church strategy ready?" Not, "Have you practiced your sermon for the day of Pentecost?"

Jesus wanted to know one thing from Peter. "Peter, do you love Me?" And He gives him three chances to answer, "Yes, Lord, I love you."

With each answer, the preciousness of Jesus comes into clearer focus. *The One who affirms me also rebukes me for my good. The One who cares about my catch also forgives me wholly. I love Him, I love Him, I love Him.* We should find encouragement from Peter's experience. Being loved by and loving Jesus *is* eternal life. Like Peter, we can have great moments of theological clarity and affection for Jesus, only to be followed by spiraling failure. Yet Jesus draws us back and pulls us close.

WHEN BAD GRAMMAR MAKES GOOD THEOLOGY

Predicates. Nominatives. Noun-verb agreement. Apposition. Modifiers. Independent and dependent clauses…

Remember these from grammar class?

The rules of grammar are intended to be the guardrails for communication. But sometimes they prevent it.

Like Peter, the apostle Paul knew well that the nature of eternal life is knowing, loving, and valuing Jesus. In his letter to the Philippians, Paul wanted to be abundantly clear as to why his heart was satisfied even as he languished under house arrest. Paul compresses all that is eternal life into a simple statement: "For to me, to live is Christ and to die is gain" (Philippians 1:21).

Now, we might have expected Paul to say something like, "For to me, to live is *serving* Christ," or "*worshipping* Christ," or "*loving* Christ." But the apostle simply says that to live *is* Christ. The grammar is awkward, but the meaning is clear—living is Christ and Christ is life.

Beyond that, the phrase contains a related gem: dying is faith giving birth to sight. If you pick up Paul's flow of thought back in verse 20, you find him talking about life and death. He expresses his deepest passion that in everything he does in life and everything associated with his death, Christ is to be central and foremost. Only when Jesus is the integrating centrality of all that we are does the threat of death evaporate with the thought that He waits for us in heaven with a prepared room (John 14:2).

When life is consumed with knowing God through Jesus, we can sincerely say, "O DEATH WHERE IS YOUR VICTORY? O DEATH WHERE IS YOUR STING?" (1 Corinthians 15:55). When dying is gain, we are unshackled from the slavish fear of it (Hebrews 2:14–15).

Eternal life is not what most people think. It is more. It is a complete redefinition and reorientation of the purpose and meaning of life itself. The same Paul who told the Philippians "to live is Christ" described this concept to the Colossians with the simple phrase "Christ, who is our life" (3:4).

Can you hear the volume level in this phrase? Jesus is our life! We began this book considering the subterranean struggles that exist beneath so many of our Christian smiles. I am convinced that these struggles are there simply because Christ is not.

We can't have faith in faith. We don't believe in belief. We don't hope in hope. Hear Jesus again: "This is eternal life, that they may know You, the only true God, and Jesus Christ whom You have sent" (John 17:3). To live is to know Jesus; to die is to be with Him forever—infinite gain!

I think this is exactly what Paul was longing for in the familiar words of his third chapter to the Philippians:

> But whatever things were gain to me, those things I have counted as loss for the sake of Christ. More than that, I count all things to be loss in view of the surpassing value of knowing Christ Jesus my Lord, for whom I have suffered the loss of all things, and count them but rubbish so that I may gain Christ, and may be found in Him, not having a righteousness of my own derived from the Law, but that which is through faith in Christ, the righteousness which comes from God on the basis of faith, that I may know

Him and the power of His resurrection and the fellowship of His sufferings, being conformed to His death; in order that I may attain to the resurrection from the dead. (vv. 7–11)

Paul wanted to experience the eternal life Jesus promised in the here and now, not just the there and then. If there's anything in your faith that isn't anchored in the person of Jesus, you're living in an eclipse. You are not enjoying the eternal life made available by the gospel. Like Lowell, you may have built a theory on a flawed assumption and missed out on the rich reality God intends for you to enjoy. He is good. He is personable. He alone can satisfy.

4

THE DISTANCE BETWEEN HEAVEN AND EARTH

During the first week of July, our planet is as far as it ever gets from the sun.

Ninety-four million miles.

That's quite a ways.

In fact it's the perfect distance. It's so perfect that the average distance of the earth from the sun is an astronomical standard of measure: a single AU, astronomical unit. Any farther and we would freeze. Closer, we fry.

This distance works for us earthlings in every way, and it is perhaps the best illustration of the greatest problem of theology. Distance and nearness. While it's wonderfully and powerfully true that "to live is Christ," there are times when He seems distant, does He not? There are times, sometimes prolonged times, when the relationship feels more like an "arrangement."

In the profoundest sense, we haven't fully understood or grasped the gospel or the intended meaning of the words *eternal life* until we've come to terms with our most pressing problem: God.

Now you might expect me to say, "Well, no, He's the solution," and we'll get to that part. But for the moment, let's wrestle with the sobering truth that man's greatest *problem* is God, God Himself. What do you do with God if He really is as the Bible describes Him? I agree with A. W. Tozer, who wrote these stirring words, "What comes into your mind when you think about God is the most important thing about you."[1] So, what does come into your mind when you think about God?

The answer ought to be, "Jesus Christ, whom He has sent," right?

But strangely, our intuition affirms what theologians, critical thinkers, and philosophers have deduced for thousands of years: mankind's basic problem is the transcendence and immanence of God. Our thoughts of Him as far away and our thoughts of Him as too close for comfort keep us forever at a fixed distance. If this seems confusing, you may be a bit lost in the lingo. Hang with me. I think the effort will clear things up.

GOD IS EVERYWHERE, ISN'T HE?

I'm the father of three boys, and this is just the kind of theologizing we might get into on a Sunday night after church over a bowl of ice cream. Some years ago we were talking about the attributes of God, specifically about God's omnipresence and omniscience. And I thought they were getting it. God is everywhere, always. You can never outrun His presence. As we're eating our ice cream, one of my sons jumped in with a question.

"Dad, God is everywhere, isn't He?"

"Yes, He is, son," I replied, thinking I might have made a mini Martin Luther out of him.

"Dad, God is, like, in our city, isn't He?"

"Yes, He is, son. He's the King." *Yep, Luther for sure, maybe a Calvin!*

"God is in our house, isn't He?"

"Yes, son." I was really feeling good about the fruits of my theological tutelage!

He furrowed his eyebrows. "God is in the room with us, isn't He?"

"Yes, He is, son."

Finally he asked, "Dad, is God in the ice cream?"

I could almost hear the balloon of my swelling pride begin to sputter. *In the ice cream?* "Well...not really."

"But you said He's everywhere."

"Well, yeah."

"But everywhere includes the ice cream, doesn't it?"

"Yes."

"Then where is God?"

"Go ask your mom!" I said. "I'm sure she can sort it out for you…"

How easy it is to push the words with which we define our theology to absurdity. How suddenly we move from soundness to silliness! The Bible presents a God who's present at every point in space, though space cannot contain Him. A God who draws near to us—in our cities, in our homes—though His very quality of being necessarily creates an unspannable distance.

Hear the psalmists sound off in this chorus of conundrums:

"Why do You stand afar off, O LORD? Why do You hide Yourself in times of trouble?" (10:1). Have you ever felt like that? *Where are You, God? I'm in trouble; I can't find You.*"

"How long, O LORD? Will You forget me forever? How long will You hide Your face from me?" (13:1). What is time to the eternal God? But time means everything to us.

"My God, my God, why have You forsaken me? Far from my deliverance are the words of my groaning" (22:1). David spoke these words originally, and then our Lord Jesus repeated some of them on the cross.

If these verses were all we understood of God, we might not care to know Him. If we put the period at the end of our theological sentence here, we might despair, and for good reason. God is transcendent. He cannot be reached and is beyond us in our petty, temporal troubles. But the chorus of Scripture continues…

The same David who lamented, *Why have You forsaken me, God? Where are You? I've looked for You in trouble; I can't find You anywhere!* also wrote Psalm 139, "Where can I go from Your Spirit? Or where can I flee from Your presence? If I ascend to heaven, You are there; if I make my bed in Sheol [death] behold, You are there. If I take the wings of the dawn, if I dwell in the remotest part of the sea, even there Your hand will lead me, and Your right hand will lay hold of me" (vv. 7–10). So which is it, David? Is He too far off to reach, or is He so close you can't evade Him?

Jeremiah also wrestled with this problem: "'Can a man hide himself in hiding places so I do not see him?' declares the LORD. 'Do I not fill the heavens and the earth?' declares the LORD" (Jeremiah 23:24).

In a different application of this very truth, Paul wrote to his dear brothers and sisters in Christ, the Philippians, "The Lord is near. Be anxious for nothing" (Philippians 4:5–6).

Reconciling these types of Scriptures is not easy. After all, this is the problem you have struggled with since the day you could reason; the record of Scripture only echoes it. The Lord is near, but He is the *Lord!* Our God is at once close and far. Immanent, transcendent.

HANDLES ON HEAVEN

As we work forward in this chapter, I want to help you understand man's core problem with God. Unless you understand this problem, you'll never see that the solution is Jesus—and you may never truly appreciate why Jesus is precious.

First we must reckon with the distance of divine transcendence; God is infinitely separated from us.

The Bible tells us that God is Spirit (John 4:24); He does not have spatial dimensions. We cannot measure Him, and consequently we cannot conceive of any limit to His presence. There's no place where He is not, but nothing can contain Him. Even at the far end of infinity and creation, if you were to explore that nothingness, God is there.

So when we speak of God's distance from us, that gulf is in reference not to space—as space is irrelevant—but to quality of being. *Transcendence* is the word that tries to measure God's majesty and holiness, how qualitatively different He is from us. To say that God is transcendent is to say that He is the King of all kings, the Lord of all lords. "Who is like the LORD our God, who is enthroned on high, who humbles Himself to behold the things that are in heaven and in the earth?" (Psalm 113:5–6).

While transcendence has to do with God's separateness, not the space or place He is in, the authors of Scripture often borrow the metaphor of height. God is Lord "in heaven above" (Deuteronomy 4:39). He has established His glory "above the heavens" (Psalm 8:1). He is "enthroned on high" (113:5). And God calls His people to exalt and give Him the highest status: "You are the LORD Most High over all the earth; You are exalted far above all gods" (97:9). Does that mean He's on a higher mountain or peering from the tallest building? No, it means He's greater in degree of person and in quality of existence. Thus it is fitting for Him to "Be exalted above the heavens, O God; Let Your glory be above all the earth" (57:5).

I love the simplicity of Solomon's declaration in Ecclesiastes 5:2: "God is in heaven and you are on the earth." That does it. You cannot get to God.

There's no ladder high enough. There's no course that makes you smart enough. He's far beyond us in His holiness, in His majesty, in the comprehensions of His mind. You can't get to Him.

In order to press any further into man's core problem with God, we must also reckon with the Bible's teaching about the nearness of divine immanence. Immanence describes God's closeness, His proximity, how His omnipresence invades your personal space. When theologians talk about God's omniscience and omnipresence, they are describing God's immanence.

Immanence accents the wonder that the transcendent God is at work—always—in all of the affairs of our lives in every part of the world. Interestingly, there are many texts that describe God's transcendence and His immanence back-to-back. For example, Moses declared, "Know therefore today, and take it to your heart, that the LORD, He is God in heaven above and on the earth below; there is no other" (Deuteronomy 4:39). "Behold, to the LORD your God belong heaven and the highest heavens, the earth and all that is in it. Yet on your fathers did the LORD set His affection to love them, and He chose their descendants after them, even you above all peoples, as it is this day" (10:14–15). God who is beyond everything chooses to condescend in love.

Even Rahab the harlot from Jericho understood this. "For the LORD your God, He is God in heaven above and on earth beneath" (Joshua 2:11). Turning to the New Testament, Paul instructed the Ephesians, "There is one body and one Spirit, just as also you were called in one hope of your calling; one Lord, one faith, one baptism, one God and Father of all who is over all and through all and in all" (Ephesians 4:4–6).

God is near and present and close in proximity. He actually holds creation together in His all-pervasive presence. "He is before all things, and in Him all things hold together" (Colossians 1:17). His divine oversight is the force that hurls electrons around nuclei and planets around stars. From the subatomic to the outer reaches of space, He is ever present.

And wonder of wonders, the One who is over us all condescends to work through us all in His body, the church! Transcendent, immanent; as hard as these may be to grasp, it is essential we consider them together.

"CONSIDER MY SERVANT, JOB"

So how do we deal with this? How do we approach a God who is too far to reach and at the same time too close to outrun? How will you deal with your God problem?

In order to understand this and spotlight the inconceivable preciousness of our Lord Jesus, consider Job, the servant of our near-far God. Job is the oldest book in the Bible—not the first chronologically, but the oldest. It was written before any other biblical record, during the time of the patriarchs. Even then, mankind perceived the great gulf between himself and God.

To read the first two chapters of Job is to experience a kind of tragedy that not even Shakespeare could write. But this is not mere literature; it really happened. This is a narrative of a deep, sudden, and seemingly meaningless blight that precipitates horrific, soul-crushing despair. But it also raises the greatest problem we have with God. *What are You thinking,*

God? What are You doing to me? Where are You in this?

Job is minding his own business, serving the Lord, loving God and walking in His ways, raising his family and enjoying the fruit of his efforts. But in a realm beyond Job's perception, a conversation happens between God and Satan.

Satan says to God, "I want to take a swing at your servant Job."

Remarkably, God answers, "Have at him."

Job would never forget that day. In rapid succession, four messengers burst through his door. These bearers of bad news must have seen each other sprinting across the field towards Job's home, each thinking he had more urgent news than the other. Out of breath and rocked with grief, none of the messengers was able to finish his report before he was cut off midsentence by another running into the room.

"The oxen and donkeys have been stolen by the Sabeans," says the first. "And they killed the servants who were working the animals!"

The second interrupts him exclaiming, "And lightning struck the sheep and their shepherds! They're all dead."

Before he can finish his sentence, messenger number three speaks over him with even greater volume, "And the Chaldeans have taken the camels, stabbing the keepers to death."

The fourth messenger silences everyone. "Your sons and daughters..." Job and his wife brace themselves for the worst. He continues, "Your sons and your daughters were eating and drinking wine in their oldest brother's house, and behold, a great wind came from across the wilderness and struck the four corners of the house, and it fell on the young people and they died, and I alone have escaped to tell you" (Job 1:18–19).

Some have speculated that Job learned of his astounding losses in all of forty-five seconds. But it got worse. Not long afterwards, he was struck with debilitating boils from the bottom of his feet to the top of his head.

Welcome to a world of pain.

In a handful of heartbeats, Job's entire world is turned inside out and upside down. We read about it, but Job lived it. Perhaps one day, when

Job reached his heavenly reward, he was granted a reading of the book that bears his name. *Ah, now it all makes sense!*

That, however, is not the story of Job.

The first two chapters merely chronicle the events. The *story*—the theological story, the story of the near-far God—begins in chapter three and goes through the remainder of the book. Job is trying to figure out how to deal with a God who is too far away to get to for an explanation and too near to ignore in his own sinful culpabilities. Job's discussions with his friends are a series of musings about the curious fact that God is both the source of and Savior from calamity.

The book of Job wrestles with the tension between God's transcendence and God's immanence, and the height of the discussion comes in chapter nine. Job has an interaction with his counselors, his friends, who are trying to sort this out with him as much as he is. Most of the counsel these friends offer him is theologically accurate, just insensitively applied.

Job begins in chapter 9, verse 2 by affirming the truism that he had just been told: God rewards the righteous and punishes the wicked. Simple enough. But then he poses the question to end all questions that points us inescapably toward the insight that contains all insight:

"But how can a man be in the right before God?"

For three verses, Job continues: "How can a man be in the right before God? If one wished to dispute with Him, He could not answer Him once in a thousand times. Wise in heart and mighty in strength, who has defied Him without harm?" (vv. 2–4). In other words, *Who has come to court with Him without being put in their place?* Next Job talks about God's immense power in creation:

It is God who removes the mountains, they know not how, when He overturns them in His anger; who shakes the earth out of its place, and its pillars tremble; who commands the sun not to shine, and sets a seal upon the stars; who alone stretches out the heavens and tramples down the waves of the sea; who makes the Bear, Orion and the Pleiades, and the chambers of the south; who does great things, unfathomable, and wondrous works without number. Were He to pass by me, I would not see Him; were He to move past me, I would not perceive Him. Were He to snatch away, who could restrain Him? Who could say to Him, "What are You doing?" (9:5–12)

In spite of the evidence that God is present and active, Job cannot perceive Him. Job sees His work in creation; he knows He's out there, but Job's senses are incapable of grasping God. Now, beginning in verse 13, he looks at God's sovereignty in judging the world:

God will not turn back His anger; beneath Him crouch the helpers of Rahab. How then can I answer Him, and choose my words before Him? For though I were right, I could not answer; I would have to implore the mercy of my judge. If I called and He answered me, I could not believe that He was listening to my voice. For He bruises me with a tempest and multiplies my wounds without cause. He will not allow me to get my breath, but saturates me with bitterness. If it is a matter of power, behold, He is the strong one! And if it is a matter of justice, who can summon Him? (vv. 13–19)

The word *summon* means "to call Him into court, to make Him give an answer." Job continues in that vein, "Though I am righteous, my mouth will condemn me" (v. 20). In other words, *Even if I try to talk about what I've done or not done, I'm still going to be bragging. I'm still going to be full of guilt! Though I am guiltless, He will declare me guilty. Though I can't see if I've done anything wrong, He certainly can find the sin in my life.*

He continues in verse 21, "I am guiltless; I do not take notice of myself; I despise my life." Job's saying, *I don't know why all this happened to me! What have I done, God?* He resigns himself to this:

51

It is all one; therefore I say, "He destroys the guiltless and the wicked." If the scourge kills suddenly, He mocks the despair of the innocent. The earth is given into the hand of the wicked; He covers the faces of its judges. If it is not He, then who is it? (vv. 22–24)

Still, he affirms God's sovereignty…

Now my days are swifter than a runner; they flee away, they see no good. They slip by like reed boats, like an eagle that swoops on its prey. Though I say, "I will forget my complaint, I will leave off my sad countenance and be cheerful," I am afraid of all my pains, I know that You will not acquit me. I am accounted wicked, why then should I toil in vain? If I should wash myself with snow and cleanse my hands with lye, yet You would plunge me into the pit, and my own clothes would abhor me. (vv. 25–31)

He's saying, *I can't fix my sin. I know I have guilt, but I don't know it all. I know I have sin, but I can't find it all. I know if You were to materialize and show Yourself, I would be guilty. But I can't figure it out! You're transcendent, God. I can't talk to You! I can't hear You!*

And then comes verses 32: "For [God] is not a man as I am that I may answer Him [talk to Him, work things out with Him], that we may go to court together." Now we must keep in mind that Job is describing an ancient near eastern court scene, not a modern court. These were very simple. The elders of a village, the wisest men, would sit together outside the city gate, and if you had an issue you needed to settle with someone, you would come before the bench and they would decide the matter.

Job says, *You're not a man, so I can't approach You in this simple, practical, customary way! You're Spirit. You're transcendent; You're way up there, hopelessly beyond me! And what's worse, You're also in my heart and condemning me! I'm totally frustrated with transcendence and immanence!*

We read the final cry of his heart beginning in verse 33. "There is no umpire between us, who may lay his hand upon us both." He pleads, "Let Him remove His rod from me, and let not dread of Him terrify me. Then I would speak and not fear Him; but I am not like that in myself" (vv. 34–35).

Job wants to sit down with God and say, *Help me understand You. Help me understand justice. Help me understand salvation. Help me understand righteousness. I just want to hear from You, God. You're too far. You're too holy. You're too awesome.*

Job is not indicting God; he's complaining because God is so wonderfully holy and majestic that he can't reason with Him as he might if God were more like himself.

If only God were, say, a man.

The thought almost seems blasphemous, to wish God was a man. Yet that is the cry of the entire Old Testament. God is *not* a man! We can't deal with God! He's Spirit! Send us an umpire!

Umpire?

The word Job uses doesn't mean "arbitrator." Job doesn't need a lawyer. He wants someone to call it like it is. Someone who could say, "Here's God; I want to represent God to you. Here's man; I want to represent you to God." There is no man who can do that! If God showed up to do this, we would be incinerated by the hot blast of His holiness!

Job is saying, *You're transcendent; I can't get to You. I can't talk to You. You're immanent; You're so close. You know everything about me. I'm condemned by Your presence. I'm undone. I wish there was some way I could talk to You through someone who would represent me rightly to You and simultaneously represent You rightly to me. Some kind of…mediator!*

That is what Job is about. Really.

Job's voice is the loudest and clearest in the chorus of Scripture on the dilemma of knowing and being known by the near-far God. And, most importantly, he points us toward the ultimate need aching in all of us. The need for some kind of umpire, some kind of mediator, who can make us right before God!

JUST WHAT THE SUFFERER ORDERED

What we need is a Who—just the One Job longed for.

In 1 Timothy 2, the answer to our core problem with God jumps out of the text. It's the mystery of divine incarnation.

We need the Holy One in our midst (see Hosea 11:9). Paul says in 1 Timothy 2:5, "There is one God, and one mediator also between God and men, the [literally "a"] man Christ Jesus." A man is the mediator between God and man!

His name is Christ Jesus.

Pastors and theologians talk so much about the deity of Christ, and with very good reason. Jesus is God, the one true, living God. Nowhere is this clearer than in the apostle John's closing words to his first epistle, "We know that the Son of God has come, and has given us understanding so that we may know Him who is true; and we are in Him who is true, in His Son Jesus Christ. This is the true God and eternal life" (1 John 5:20). We love talking about the deity of our Savior.

But we cannot lose sight of the fact that Jesus is also a man. A human. Flesh, bone, and blood. This is the mystery of the divine incarnation. The incarnation is not God minus anything. It is God plus humanity. Jesus is fully God and truly man.

Read Hebrews 2:14–18 for the reasoning behind this mysterious wonder:

> Therefore, since the children share in flesh and blood, He Himself likewise also partook of the same, that through death He might render powerless him who had the power of death, that is, the devil, and might free those who through fear of death were subject to slavery all their lives. For assuredly He does not give help to angels, but He gives help to the descendants of Abraham. Therefore, He had to be made like His brethren in all things, so that He might become a merciful and faithful high priest in things pertaining to God, to make propitiation for the sins of

the people. For since He Himself was tempted in that which He has suffered, He is able to come to the aid of those who are tempted.

Here is a Mediator who understands the majestic splendor of God and the helpless predicament of man. But the reality of Jesus the Mediator was much more than the suffering patriarch imagined. Jesus died to free us from the sting and fear of death. Jesus lived a human life to be a sympathetic, understanding, merciful High Priest for His children. But this Priest did not perform sacrifices; He *was* the ultimate, final sacrifice for the sins of all who would believe.

Two chapters later, the writer to the Hebrews further explained the miraculous, amazing benefits of the Incarnation:

> Therefore, since we have a great high priest who has passed through the heavens, Jesus the Son of God, let us hold fast our confession. For we do not have a high priest who cannot sympathize with our weaknesses, but One who has been tempted in all things as *we are, yet* without sin. Therefore let us draw near with confidence to the throne of grace, so that we may receive mercy and find grace to help in time of need. (Hebrews 4:14–16)

He passed through the heavens and stopped in here. Read Matthew, Mark, Luke, and John, and you encounter the almighty God walking on Israel's dusty roads. Job wanted to meet God in a court where each party could be represented by a Mediator. This request was granted on behalf of all mankind just outside the northwest wall of Jerusalem, on a hill called the Skull, on a primitive execution device called a cross. But the strangest thing happened at this court proceeding at Calvary. Instead of both parties meeting together to work things out through the Mediator, they both abandoned Him.

Judas betrayed Him. The disciples fled for their lives. Peter denied Him three times. Worse, the Father Himself abandoned Him to horrific crucifixion and sinful punishment. In Gethsemane Jesus prayed to His Heavenly Father and received no answer. He hung on the cross and for the first time, in a mysterious intertrinitarian sense, experienced divine transcendence! "My God, My God, why have You forsaken Me?" (Matthew 27:46). At the point of the verdict in the courtroom, both the Father and the men He was dying for left Him. He alone bore the rejection. He alone bore the wrath. As a result, He alone bears the reward for all who place faith in Him.

Do you comprehend the treasure we have in Jesus? He understands life here because He's been tempted in every way like us. He knows everything we face. He knows the world. He knows suffering. He knows pain. When He prays for us (Romans 8:34), when He intercedes for us, He gets it.

And at the right time, the near-far God straightened the question mark that befuddled humanity into an exclamation point following the death of His own Son.

This One will be your Mediator!

Jesus alone spans the distance between heaven and earth. He offers His nail-scarred hands to those who want to draw close to the faraway God. For those who feel their need for God and those who are wounded by this world, He suffered divine abandonment so that we would not have to.

Jesus entered the dark eclipse to bring us to God, to make us "light in the Lord" (Ephesians 5:8).

5

STARING AT THE SON

Jesus was spending a final meal with His disciples in the Upper Room of the house He'd secured for just the occasion.

He was hours away from being rejected by them, even as He blessed the meal of His life for theirs.

He was hours away from arrest, hours from condemnation, and just a few more hours from execution—the cross.

Of the twenty-one chapters that John the apostle penned in his gospel account, five describe what Jesus said and did at this last supper. John, leaning close, heard everything.

Unthinkably, Jesus was going away.

Unimaginably, it was going to be for the best.

Of chief concern to John's closest friend and Lord was His relationship with them *after* His resurrection. In that Upper Room, Jesus answered the questions none of them were yet asking. He knew that future generations of His disciples, struggling to simply and purely fellowship with Him in the Son-eclipsed world, would learn to hang on every word, for His words are life.

At the head of this list of all-important questions nobody was asking was this: How do I live with, how do I live for, how can I experience an *invisible* Savior?

Jesus was aware that after His resurrection and ascension, the disciples would be coping with how to have a relationship with Him when He wasn't there physically. So He tells them with great compassion, "I will not leave you as orphans; I will come to you" (John 14:18). Now we understand from the rest of the New Testament, especially the book of Acts, that Jesus would return to earth to manifest Himself to the disciples and many others after His resurrection. However, Jesus left them again after that, when He returned to heaven. Three verses later, Jesus elaborates on His mind-bending plan to remain with them powerfully and richly. He says, "He who has My commandments and keeps them is the one who loves Me; and he who loves Me will be loved by My Father, and I will love him and will disclose Myself to him" (v. 21).

Consider that last phrase. Jesus promises to disclose Himself. The Greek word is *emphanidzo,* meaning "manifest, appear, make known." What kind of disclosure is Jesus describing?

Well, first of all, let's answer what it doesn't mean. It doesn't mean that Jesus is going to show up in bodily form or in some kind of a mystical vision to believers. No, there's far more to this. What Jesus is promising transcends a momentary encounter, some fleeting experience. To those who obey the Word and love the Lord, Jesus offers what's most needful.

James Boice describes Christ's marvelous offer to us so well: "Having come to know who Jesus is and having believed on Him, the Christian will then want to know Him more fully. In this case, the knowledge will not be so much a knowledge *about* Him leading to a faith, but rather a deep knowledge *of* Him in which the disciple comes to experience the Lord in the fullest most personal way."[1]

Jesus is promising an experience here! The question is, how can a Christian love and be loved by an unseen Christ such that they might enter into this experience? Boice goes on, "How then, would He be seen? The answer is that He would be seen in a spiritual sense, as through the revelation of Himself in the Bible and through the Holy Spirit's witness to that revelation within the hearts of the disciples and their followers. He is made vividly real. This sounds like fantasy to those who have not been born again, but to those who have been made alive by God's Spirit, the presence of Christ is more real than anything they see physically, more real than even their own hands or feet."[2]

So here's my question. Do you experience that, or does it sound like…fantasy…just more Christianspeak?

Listen again to the promise in John 14:21: "He who has My commandments and keeps them is the one who loves Me; and he who loves Me will be loved by My Father, *and I will love him and will disclose Myself to him.*"

Put simply, this verse tells us that if we will remove the eclipse of disobedience and apathy, something special will happen in our walk with Christ. Paul hints at this in 2 Corinthians 3:18, where he writes, "But we all, with unveiled face, beholding as in a mirror the glory of the Lord, are being transformed into the same image from glory to glory, just as from the Lord, the Spirit." In other words, we see Christ now, and the more we know Him and the more we study Him, the more we become like the clear image we see of Him.

Looking for and seeing and gazing at the excellencies, the glories of Jesus leads to greater vision, sharper focus, deeper awareness of Jesus and His permanent abiding presence. It elevates the soul to a higher vantage point of worship.

We must learn to stare at the Son of God such that we are blinded to all the allurements of the world! All encumbrances aside, all slackheartedness aside, everything aside but…

Him.

If we would know the fullness of this disclosure of Himself that Christ described at that supper table, our lives would be wholly and enduringly different.

ECLIPSED STILL

So why does the eclipse persist? Why do our toes and fingers seem so much more immanently real than this fellowship with Jesus? It's because there are qualifications for seeing the Son and enjoying this manifestation of Himself to us. Suppose you lie in bed and wonder to yourself, *I'm pretty sure this is real. I'm pretty sure I believe this. I have assurance sometimes. I'm looking around at everyone else; they seem to have it down, but I'm not so sure.* The question is, *Have you qualified for that experience with Jesus?*

Jesus longs to and has promised to manifest Himself to believers if, first of all, they obey. As we saw above, His words of that night reverberate through the ages and pierce us still: "He who has My commandments and keeps them is the one who loves Me" (John 14:21).

How effortless it is to breathe out that familiar Christian declaration: "I love Jesus!" How easy it is to sing love songs to the Savior.

But the proof is in the doing. "Having" His commandments means knowing them; "keeping" His commandments means obeying them. It's not unique to this verse. Further along Jesus said, "If anyone loves Me, he will keep My word; and My Father will love him, and We will come and make Our abode with him" (v. 23). This manifestation will be a permanent, ongoing experience to those who are obedient! And in 15:10–11 the Lord restates and amplifies this principle, saying, "If you keep My commandments, you will abide in My love; just as I have kept My Father's commandments and abide in His love. These things I have spoken to you so that My joy may be in you, and that your joy may be made full." There it is! Manifestations of Christ are the equivalent of having our joy filled up, where we're overwhelmed, exulting, enjoying Christ, loving the fact that we've been saved, loving the person of Jesus.

True Christians are distinguished from unbelievers as well as from nominal Christians by their obedience to Christ.

In 1 John 2:3–6 John must have been reminded of Jesus' Upper Room Discourse as he wrote, "By this we know that we have come to know Him, if we keep His commandments." So confidence and assurance are predicated on obedience. Then he gives us a practical illustration. "The one who says, 'I have come to know Him,' and does not keep His commandments, is a liar, and the truth is not in him; but whoever keeps His word, in him the love of God has truly been perfected. By this we know that we are in Him: the one who says he abides in Him ought himself to walk in the same manner as He walked." Jesus issued many commands during His earthly ministry, but this verse also tells us that the very life of Jesus—His conversations, His interactions, His questions, His answers— all of those become obeyable examples.

We must set ourselves to study the Scriptures and to obey all that Christ is revealed to be in them because sin dampens our affections and dulls our souls to our only hope of satisfaction. Sin is the moon that eclipses the Son. You will never have any prospect of experiencing the presence of Jesus promised in John 14:21 unless your life is set on a course of obedience. Sin will obscure the glory of Christ and you'll plod forward in that nightish day of semi-Christianity, a shadowland of discouraging uncertainty.

There's a second qualification if we would experience this disclosure of Christ: love. John 14:21 tells us that love is defined by obedience, but then Jesus goes on to say, "And he who loves Me will be loved by My Father, and I will love him." It's a workhorse word in the New Testament: *agape*, a commitment of inclination. So what does it mean to love Jesus? Yes, we've already seen obedience. That's a given. But true Christians are distinguished from unbelievers not only by their obedience, but by their love for Christ.

Let this question echo in your soul: Do you love Christ? Is He precious to you, as He was to Peter? Is He the hub of your faith and your life, or have you made Christianity something of a way to live instead of a Person to love? This is a concept we talk about but don't often analyze. Let's use the Scriptures to break this love down into its essentials.

LOVE AND FAITH

First of all, love beholds the Son with eyes of faith. What is faith? John 1:12 states, "But as many as received Him, to them He gave the right to become children of God, to those who believe in His name." The "name" describes all of who Jesus is. We affirm all that He did and all that He is. To receive Christ means being persuaded that Jesus and the gospel are true. Have you really come to a settled confidence that the gospel is true, that Jesus is true, that the biblical narrative of His life is true? Have you separated your thoughts about Jesus and your thoughts about Scripture and your thoughts about the gospel from the computer-generated graphics you see in the movie theaters? From the mythology you read in freshman literature?

The author of Hebrews describes faith as "the assurance of things hoped for, the conviction of things not seen" (11:1). Sight won't help you see the Son. Sight will show you the world, but it cannot show you Him. To see Jesus, you need to believe.

I'll never forget a guy in high school I was trying to share the gospel with. Over and over and over we discussed this matter of faith. Finally he came back and said, "It's not true. It is not true."

And I said, "What do you mean it's not true?"

He said, "I proved God's not there last night. I laid in my bed and I was thinking about what you said, and I was thinking about Jesus and the cross and whether He really raised from the dead or not. And so I turned my lamp on. And I said, 'God if you're real, wiggle the curtain.' I waited and I waited and I waited and God never wiggled the curtain. If He's so powerful, if He's really there, He should have wiggled the curtain." Sadly, he was serious. He had proposed an inane test for the God of the universe to establish His existence.

That is not faith. The apostle John reversed my friend's test. He wrote, "But as many as received Him, to them He gave the right to become children of God, even to those who believe in His name" (John 1:12), not to "those who *saw* who He was."

Faith is the eye of the soul. Here is a way to understand it: you have an eye of faith. That faith looks through the lens of Scripture. And the light that makes this sight of faith possible is the Holy Spirit's illumination. An eye of faith, a lens of Scripture, the light of the illumination of the Holy Spirit. Suddenly the Bible comes alive and we see Christ's excellence, His splendor!

There must be faith that engages with God's Word on Jesus and estimates it to be the most important information in the world.

There's nothing more important to you than the truth of Scripture. You can study your calculus and pass the test. You can study all your history facts and pass that test. And this may increase your knowledge of events, your understanding of processes.

But it doesn't touch your soul.

Jesus is the pearl of great price, the treasure worth every sacrifice (Matthew 13:44–46). He's the one Paul ached for in Philippians 3—"that I may know Him." I think Paul was asking for the very manifestation that we've been talking about in this chapter, the one that Jesus promised in John 14:21. Paul longed for others to experience this as well. Ephesians 1:15–18 is his prayer: "For this reason I too, having heard of the faith in the Lord Jesus which exists among you and your love for all the saints, do not cease giving thanks for you, while making mention of you in my prayers; that the God of our Lord Jesus Christ, the Father of glory, may give to you a *spirit of wisdom and of revelation in the knowledge of Him*. I pray that the eyes of your heart may be enlightened." Paul is asking God to enable them to see Jesus with the "eyes of your heart," that "the spirit of wisdom and of revelation" would shine His light in their souls.

Peter also picks up this theme. First Peter 1:8–9 says, "And though you have not seen Him, you love Him, and though you do not see Him now, but believe in Him, you greatly rejoice with joy inexpressible and full of glory, obtaining as the outcome of your faith the salvation of your souls." No one to whom Peter was writing had ever seen Jesus with physical eyes, yet Peter encourages us that faith in and love for Jesus without the senses leads to inexpressible joy! Faith opens the way to love for the Savior, and joy echoes back upon our souls.

Has faith in Jesus connected you with inexpressible joy? Or do you live in the eclipse of the Son by doubt, fear, condemnation, and questions?

In 1677, Thomas Vincent wrote:

The essence of Christianity consists in believing. Reason makes us men, but faith makes us true Christians.[3] If you would attain this love unto Jesus Christ, whom you have never seen, you must get a thorough persuasion that there is such a person as Jesus Christ, and that He is such a person indeed as the Scriptures have revealed Him to be. The reason why heathens and infidels are without love to Christ is because they have never heard of Him; and the reason many nominal Christians that have heard of Christ are without love to Him is because they are not really persuaded that there is, or ever was, such a person Jesus Christ in the world. If you would attain this love, you must give a firm assent to this truth (which is the greatest of all, and the very pillar and foundation of the whole Christian religion), that Christ really is, and the history of Him is no cunningly devised fable.[4]

No one can claim that faith is easy. We can all identify with the honest father who responded to Jesus: "I do believe; help my unbelief," in Mark 9:24. Though his son has just been healed, he longed for more of the strength that faith gives. Even the disciples asked the Lord in Luke 17:5, "Increase our faith!" If even the disciples needed their faith increased, Paul's prayer that "the eyes of your heart may be enlightened" makes perfect sense.

LOVE AND UNDERSTANDING

Love also longs to understand Christ, to "know Him." Love craves knowledge of its Beloved. It is impossible to overstate how important the knowledge of Christ is to loving Him. The less we know about Him, the less air flows into the lungs of our souls. The more we inform our minds with truth about Jesus, the more captivated we become with wonder of the God-man. Knowledge of the Savior provides an authentic, rational encounter with divine majesty.

Peter wrote, "Grace and peace be multiplied to you in the knowledge of God and of Jesus our Lord; seeing that His divine power has granted to us everything pertaining to life and godliness, through the true knowledge of Him who called us by His own glory and excellence" (2 Peter 1:2–3). Peter understood that the reception and experience of grace and peace are the consequences of the knowledge of God and Jesus our Lord. Beyond that, this knowledge grants us all, everything we need for living life and being godly. Everything our soul desires comes from understanding Jesus.

Sometimes—too often—we want other things, but Peter gives us a clear hint that if our souls recognize the spiritual needs that the knowledge of Jesus meets, then He will become the object of our desire. The truth is, what you want and what you need *is* Jesus, but you won't know that until you know Him. The more intensely He becomes the focused centrality of our faith, the more His worth overshadows all other joys.

Paul makes the same connection in Ephesians. He prays "that Christ may dwell in your hearts through faith; that you, being rooted and grounded in love, may be able to *comprehend* with all the saints what is the breadth and length and height and depth, and *to know the love of Christ which surpasses knowledge*, that you may be filled up to all the fullness of God" (3:17–19).

Did you catch that strange turn of phrase? —"to know the love of Christ which surpasses knowledge." Sounds like a conundrum, a paradox, an impossibility. What does it mean to comprehend and know something beyond knowing? The key is seeing how Paul triangulates three points: comprehension, knowledge, and *love*. The goal is to be filled up to all the fullness of God by knowing the love of Christ (v. 19). The experience of Jesus' love for us and our love for Him is the catapult for "getting it" in the Christian faith.

Have you been catapulted into the knowledge of Jesus?

Have you marinated in the depth of His love for you?

Knowledge leads to comprehension; comprehension leads to understanding; understanding feeds love for Christ.

LOVE AND AFFECTIONS

We stare at the Son by faith, as our love for Him grows with our knowledge. What does that mean emotionally and experientially? We touched on this in chapter two, but it's time to make a further connection.

Love for Jesus induces devotion and affections. Most of us are familiar with what devotion is: dedication, loyalty, attachment. But what are affections? This question was at the heart of a significant theological debate during the Great Awakening. During that time people were being converted, repenting from sins, and some were having emotional manifestations of their faith. The intensity of these responses raised suspicion about their authenticity. In response, Jonathan Edwards wrote a book that examined the validity of these experiences. It would become a Christian classic entitled *Religious Affections*.

Edwards defines *affections* as, "no other than the more vigorous and sensible exercises of the inclination and will of the soul." In other words, the affections are the leanings of the soul. It is that part of you that longs for something, that asks for something, that is attracted to something.

At the end of the first section of *Religious Affections,* Edwards writes:

[I]s there anything which Christians can find in heaven or earth so worthy to be the objects of their admiration and love, their earnest and longing desires, their hope, and their rejoicing, and their fervent zeal, as those things that are held forth to us in the gospel of Jesus Christ?… God [has] disposed things, in the affair of our redemption, and in his glorious dispensations, revealed to us in the gospel, as though everything were purposely contrived in such a manner, as to have the greatest possible tendency to reach our hearts in the most tender part, and move our affections most sensibly and strongly. How great cause have we therefore to be humbled to the dust, that we are no more affected![5]

Slow reading, but there's rich truth here. The whole reason you have affections is to enjoy Christ. And everything recorded about Christ in Scripture was specifically put there to draw out your affections, to discover His attractiveness, to make your love more deep and intimate. What does it look like when our love for Jesus controls our affections? He Himself will be the object and focus of our love; our hopes will long for Him; our desire will be for Him; our hate and anger will be directed at sin because it offends Him. All the powers and aspirations of the heart will look to Him. Thoughts of Him will be our favorite thoughts. Remembrances of Him will be our most precious memories. Our consciences will be tuned to His heart. Every sense and ability will be at His disposal:

eyes to see His glory,

ears to hear His word,

tongues to proclaim His praise,

feet to serve His mission,

awareness to give Him attention.

Our gifts will be used for Him, our talents displayed for His glory. Our resources and possessions will all be at His disposal. Every relationship will be regulated by our greater love for Him. Every moment of life will be about Jesus. He will come to have first place in everything (Colossians 1:18).

True love for Jesus will then control all our human affections.

Perhaps you're thinking I have fast-forwarded to heaven. *Hold on. We're not ready for this!* But what then will you do with the clear teaching of Jesus, and of Peter and Paul and John? If we obey and love Jesus, He will manifest Himself to us by giving us affections for Him and deepening our comprehension and vision of His beauty and excellence.

Our eyes of faith can see Him, and that's all it takes to get started.

Now it's time to step into the broad rays of Christ's glory until His beauty and His wonder satisfy you. Stare, long and hard, at the Son.

6

THE WORD
AND WORDS

Some of us, in our heart of hearts, wish we lived in Old Testament times, the good ol' days with Moses.

We have trouble getting jazzed about a mysterious communion with an invisible Jesus in a world of faith, no matter how great it promises to be. We want an experience, a tangible display of God. Right now. And preferably in high definition.

As such, we're in good company. Moses had the same issues, and the people whom he led had it pretty easy in a lot of ways.

In those days you didn't have to pray about God's will. You just woke up in the morning and fell in behind old faithful, the pillar of cloud. It was pretty hard to miss this giant tornado rolling across the land. By night they had the same routine only they were led by a different sort of pillar, a giant tower of fire. They knew that God was with them. They knew exactly where God was leading them from moment to moment. They knew which way to go in the canyon. They knew which way to go across the open plain and in the desert. They just followed this big, unmistakable, unmissable, impossible-to-argue-with, -evade, or -ignore manifestation of God.

Easy enough.

Well, because of their ongoing sin, God ultimately took that leading presence away. It was good while it lasted...

Without their divine GPS, as we all know, they wandered around in the wilderness for decades and decades—an entire generation made cranky from being forever stuck in traffic in the middle of nowhere. After that, God promised to continue to lead His people through Moses. To facilitate this, God set up a tent of meeting. We read about it in Exodus 33.

Moses is to set up this tent outside of the camp, go into it, and speak to God "face to face, just as a man speaks to his friend" (v. 11). Truly, this was an amazing privilege, but it wasn't enough for Moses. That was an encounter, a momentary experience, but Moses wanted something that lasted, something that revealed to him personally more of the glory and power that he knew God held. So in 33:18 he says, "'I pray You, *show me Your glory!*'" Moses appealed to God to reveal Himself in the most immediate sense he knew—sight. *Show me Your glory. I want to see You, God. To see You is to know You. Show me who You are; show me Your essence.*

As Moses waited in faith for God to flip on the light switch and pull back the curtains, the suspense must have been killing him! *This is it! A glimpse at this Holy One whom I have served and worshipped for all these long years in the desert!* But God's answer to Moses would reveal to him—and to all the readers of this record down through the ages—more than Moses could have dreamed. Verse 19 continues unapologetically: "And He said, 'I Myself will make all My goodness [a synonym for glory] pass before you, and *will proclaim* the name of the LORD before you.'"

Note the subtle switch here...

Moses: "Show me who You are!"

God: "I will proclaim to you who I am!"

Moses: "I want to *see* You."

God: "I want you to *hear* Me."

Moses asked for something to *see* when he wanted to know God better; God gave him something to *hear* instead. Moses wanted to catch a vision that would so transfix and enrapture and satisfy his soul that he would never question the power and pure glory of his God again. But God in His infinite wisdom gave Moses—and all of us—His enduring and perfect words.

In the moments that followed, God proclaimed His name in the richest and most explicit sequence of theologically charged words ever heard up to that instant in history. In them we find an unsurpassed definition of the character of the person of the living God that subsequent authors of Scripture would hearken back to as simply, "the Name."

Moses asked to see; God elected to proclaim. God is fundamentally verbal.

We see the same phenomenon when God speaks to Samuel, a young man who is dedicated to serving in the tabernacle. In the middle of the night he hears something and thinks it's Eli, his boss, talking to him. He wakes to the sound of his name, "Samuel..."

He rises and replies, "What do you want, Eli?"

This happens a few times, and finally Eli tells him, "I'm not saying anything! If you're hearing a voice, I think it's God." This was a time when hearing the word of the Lord was rare in Israel, but at the end of the account in 1 Samuel 3:21, we read, "And the LORD appeared again at Shiloh, because the LORD revealed Himself to Samuel at Shiloh by the *word of the LORD*." Just as He had to Moses, God appeared to Samuel by a sure and perfect word. The Lord says in essence, *Samuel, do you want to understand who I am? Listen to me!*

Why did God choose to whisper to Samuel in the night, rather than appear in a blazing vision of glory? Because God wanted Samuel to live by faith, to prove His word throughout the course of his life, as indeed he did. First Samuel 3:19 reads, "Thus Samuel grew and the LORD was with him and let none of his words fail." Not a fleeting and transient experience, but a faith-sustaining word was what Samuel required. Hearing God's Word triggers a response of faith that seeing cannot. Hebrews 11:1 says, "Now faith is the assurance of things hoped for, the conviction of things not seen." Faith is fed by hearing and by reading, not by watching and by seeing.

FILLED BY FAITH

Faith fills our hearts with an understanding of God from His Word that encourages us to keep on seeking and believing. Several years ago, we made a significant mistake when calculating our tax withholdings and actually had a good tax day! I said to my wife, Kim, "Honey, what do you want to do?" She began to list some options: We could pay this off; we could do this or that.

I had just finished my terminal degree. She had sacrificed much to help me finish school, so I said, "What if I took you to Hawaii as a thank-you for serving me as I finished school?"

She prayed and fasted for about two seconds and said, "Great!" So, nearly a year in advance, we began dreaming and scheming and planning and praying and brochuring and web surfing all that we could about Hawaii. We were so excited. Though we had never been there, we steeped ourselves in facts about Hawaii—what it was like, what was happening there, what we would experience there. But even more than all of that, I was excited about who I would be with: my bride. We would get to do all of this together.

We were living by faith and getting excited about a place we had never been. On a much grander scale, this is how faith works in the Bible. When you allow the truths and promises of Scripture to fill your heart and take control of your life, the here and now become bearable, even inconsequential. His words won't fail us. His words are all that are required to know this God and the abundant life He offers.

JUST ONE WORD

God presents Himself to us in words. And this verbal God who Himself invented language has chosen only one Word, His favorite Word, with which to do so. We learn this at the outset of John's Gospel, in verses familiar to us all: "In the beginning was the Word, and the Word was with God, and the Word was God. He [the Word] was in the beginning with God. All things came into being through Him, and apart from Him nothing came into being that has come into being" (vv. 1–3).

Nothing has come into being without this Word. Now the question is, "What is this Word?" The Jews were very familiar with what the word *word* meant, because the "Word" was usually associated with God. "The Word of the LORD came…" is the refrain of the entire Old Testament. It's not a complicated concept. What do words do? They communicate. They transmit ideas. They reveal what someone is thinking.

In the beginning was the Communication—what God wanted us to know about Himself. Everything, singly and totally, God wanted to express to us about Himself. But this Communication is not an abstract thought, like the Greek notion of the "logos." This Communication is not an *it*, but a *He*. "*He* was in the beginning with God" (v. 2). The "Word" is a He, and He is God.

To further expound on this, John makes it clear that the Word, the Communication, the what-God-wanted-us-to know-about-Himself, became a man. He "became flesh, and dwelt among us" (v. 14). The Word was God; the Word became a man, and yet verse 18 continues, "No one has seen God at any time."

John appears to contradict himself here. If the Word walked among us and we have seen Him and His glory, how can the apostle tell us that no one has seen God at any time? The next phrase in verse 18 clarifies, "the only begotten God who is in the bosom of the Father, He has explained *Him*." The Word from God explains the Father. The Father Himself remains unseen. That's how Paul described this same thing to the Colossians: "He is the image of the invisible God" (1:15).

Now to understand that in a very simple way, the author of Hebrews says this: "God, after He spoke long ago to the fathers in the prophets in many portions and in many ways, in these last days has spoken to us in His Son" (1:1–2). For the rest of the chapter, the writer goes on to describe how Jesus is higher than the angels. The Greek rendering of that precious phrase in verse 2 reads, "In these last days has spoken to us *in Son*." In other words, God spoke to us in the language of His Son. God's one-word language is Jesus. In that term, you know all that God wants you to know about Himself. The national anthem of Heaven has a one-word lyric: Jesus. Think about it.

"In Son."

Do you speak Son? The incarnation is God's best, clearest, most perfect language. Have you, singly and totally, comprehensively and exclusively, received that Communication? Have you, like Moses and Samuel, ceased pursuing some fleeting experience and instead begun to build your life upon His revelation?

THE BOOK IS ALWAYS BETTER

God wrote a book. True, it's a book that describes just one Word—Jesus—but still God authored His book, the Bible. The question that's incumbent upon us is: What is this book? You've been told by parents, pastors, spiritual leaders, and disciplers, "Hey, go read the Bible."

So you jump in and you start reading. *Wow! Genesis 1 and 2, Creation; Genesis 3, the Fall; Genesis 4, murder; this is getting interesting....*

Genesis 5 and 6, some genealogies, the flood; kind of interesting. You get into Abraham, Isaac, Jacob, and Joseph. *Exodus, I saw the movie.* Then you get to Leviticus and it gets gory. Then the book of Numbers, and there's a lot of...numbers.

But what is this book? Well, the book has two testaments: an older testament and a newer testament. The Old Testament is the history of man's need for salvation by faith. It also lays the foundation of God as a gracious God demonstrating kindness and patience, especially to those who believe.

The message of the Old Testament is that we're in trouble with God because of our sin and we need a Savior. As we talked about in chapter 4, we are left to lament with Job that there is no mediator—we can't find a Savior ourselves (Job 9:33). How can we be made right with God?

The New Testament answers that question. The message of the New Testament is that we have a Savior and it's Jesus. Who Jesus is, what He's done, what it means to know Him, what the future holds for believers after death: this is the stuff of the New Testament. The Bible paints the portrait of Jesus on your mind's canvas.

My youngest son loves to read. It's a lot of fun to watch him read. When he reads something funny, he smiles. When something is a bit tense, his eyebrows go up. I love his love for reading. One of his favorite books was recently adapted into a film. He was super excited to see it. One night our family took him. We sat there and watched him as much as the movie. Afterward we went out for a snack.

Before I could ask him what he thought about the movie, he passionately blurted out, "I like the book better than the movie!"

"Why?" I asked.

"Because what I saw in my mind was better than what I saw on the screen."

What a great insight when applied to the Bible, I thought. By the illumination of the Holy Spirit, the words come alive in our minds and hearts as we meditate on the realities they describe. God left us a book, not a DVD series. He has not shortchanged us in giving us a book because the book reveals His Son. And it's better than any movie.

FROZEN IN

Think of how God revealed His book. It's not like any other volume. It begins with, well, the beginning. But what follows is a bit unexpected. God did not leave us a how-to manual or a treatise on systematic theology. Instead He framed His revelation of Himself in real-life dramas. He froze His truth in cultures and contexts, in language and time, in history and geography. He communicated His revelation in real lives through real encounters with Himself: stories, prophets and prophecies, histories, good guys and bad guys, miraculous events, commandments, and proclamations about His person. Ultimately, that is what the Bible is, the record of God's revelation of Himself.

The fullness of God, the immensity of His character, the majesty of

His splendor, the mystery of His likeness is all known in Jesus (Colossians 2:2). "In Him all the fullness of Deity dwells in bodily form" (v. 9). "He is the image of the invisible God" (1:15). "He is the radiance of [God's] glory and the exact representation of His nature" (Hebrews 1:3).

On a seven-mile stretch of road between Jerusalem and Emmaus, the resurrected Jesus met a man named Cleopas and his friend who were deep and heavy in conversation. They were discussing the events surrounding a man from Nazareth who had disrupted and dominated the Passover celebration the week before. After traveling with them a while, Jesus revealed His identity. Imagine their shock when they saw that the man publicly executed and buried was the one walking and talking with them! Jesus knew they needed the whole story, so he "explained to them the things concerning Himself *in all the Scriptures*" (Luke 24:27). There it is! The Scriptures concern themselves with Jesus. The Bible is the revelation of God. And the clearest word about God is Jesus.

TAKING EFFECT

Let's ask the question that is begged. How does reading words on a page from an ancient document change your life? Why is it that some people read this book and it makes no difference, and others read it and their lives are radically transformed?

I remember taking a class in college called The Bible as English Literature and thinking, *Oh, great! I'm going to learn the Bible!* Little did I know that it would be a whole semester of the instructor trying to convince us that the Bible wasn't written by God, nor was it written by the authors named in the biblical text itself. According to this PhD, the Bible is a beautifully written literary work with some nice advice, but utterly unreliable as a source of truth.

Again, how is it that some read the Bible and it has a certain effect, while others read it and there's no effect? For a believer, reading or hearing the truth of God in the Bible puts divinely inspired data in your mind. When you receive its content as the living, active word of the living God

(Hebrews 4:12), something supernatural happens. This volume is not like any other book. The truth in the Bible is rationally perceived by your mind and absorbed by your soul like water soaking into a dry sponge, *if* God has prepared you.

In 1 Corinthians 2:14–15, Paul says, "But a natural man does not accept the things of the Spirit of God, for they are foolishness to him; and he cannot understand them, because they are spiritually appraised. But he who is spiritual appraises all things, yet he himself is appraised by no one." Where are the "things of the Spirit of God"? They're contained in the Bible. The natural man, the unconverted mind, does not accept the things of God. They're a joke to him, a delusion. A Christian, however, "appraises all things" in the Word of God, "yet he himself is appraised by no one." In other words, the world looks at him as a fool while God looks at him as one who's had his eyes opened and can understand His book.

So what should you do when you sit down with your Bible to appraise its truth and apply it? Some believers are bent on reading the Bible through in a year. While that could be a great discipline, let me add another element. At some point in your Christian experience you need to learn to read with slow, concentrated purpose, intentionally expecting to hear God's voice. It is all too easy to read multiple chapters of Scripture at racehorse pace only to finish and wonder what you just read. With this, there is sometimes a temptation to treat God's precious Book as a magic good-luck charm to bring good fortune and God's blessing into your life. Yes, God blesses the reading of His Word, but there is so much more.

God has designed His truth to engage our minds in meditation in such a way that our imaginations are tuned to His divine frequency. When you read the Bible, let your imagination wrap itself around the realities of its pages. If you're reading the account of Jesus walking on the water in the storm, stop and hear the thunder and see the lightning. Feel the boat with its open deck being tossed to and fro, rocking and rolling to the edge of capsizing. Search in vain for the shore only to find another set of crashing waves. Look at the terror on the disciples' faces as they hold on to the boat and one another. Let the panic of that scene grip your imagination. Let your mind engage the story. Saturate your thinking with biblical data until it feeds and floods your imagination. I think that's why God gave us the imagination: to think deeply and long about biblical truth.

The same type of meditation works in material that is not narrative. Read the words "For by grace you have been saved through faith" from Ephesians 2:8. Now consider… *For by grace I've been saved. Salvation came because of God giving me something I didn't deserve. How did I get that? I'm saved? From what? How did that happen? Through faith, through believing what I can't see.* And you start going through all the different layers of blessings in those few words.

Don't read so you can check off the box for the day's reading. Read on purpose. Read to understand God in Christ.

AWARENESS OF GOD'S WAYS AND WAY

As you read God's Word, cultivate awareness so that the truth you just read lasts beyond the devotions. "Teach me your ways," Moses said, "so I may know you" (Exodus 33:13, NIV). Remarkably, this request follows the scene where Moses sat in a tent and spoke to God face to face, as a man speaks to his friend. But he wanted more. He desired to know God beyond the tent experience, as good as that was. In our terms, he wanted to know God beyond the devotional time. Moses gives us an amazing insight into how this happens by the request he makes.

"Teach me your ways so I may *know you."* Moses knew that if he understood the ways of God from the past, he would know how to walk with God in the present. What are the ways of God? God's predictable patterns of behavior, the paths He travels. God is immutable; He does not change. To grasp God's ways in the Bible is to know His ways in your life, today. But there is more.

During a needed retreat from the crowds in Galilee, Jesus took Peter, James, and John up on a mountain in Caesarea Philippi for a surprise. At the top where there was little chance for interruption, He was physically transfigured and they caught a glimpse of the glory of the Son of God (Matthew 17:1–8; 2 Peter 1:16–18). Interestingly, Moses and Elijah showed up and had a conversation with the Lord. If we could have interviewed Moses, he would have said something like, "I asked God if I could know Him by knowing His ways. However, Jesus is the best way to know the Father!" In fact Jesus Himself said, "I am the way, and the truth, and the life; no one comes to the Father but through Me" (John 14:6).

The best way to know God is to know Jesus. And the only way to know Jesus is through the written Word of God.

TRUST THE BOOK

Do you believe the foundational truth that God does not have a speech impediment? He doesn't lisp. He doesn't stutter. He doesn't have an accent so thick He's too difficult to understand. He doesn't stammer. He never hesitates. He does not work up the nerve to say difficult things. And He does not neglect to say anything encouraging. God has none of the problems we have as human communicators—none.

Scripture's pages are the only way you're going to find understanding of Jesus. The Bible is the only pen that can trace the face of Christ on the soul's page. The Word of God is Jesus Christ. And the Word of God is the Bible which points to and explains Him. Read the Bible as God intends, and you will discover Jesus.

In his book *The True Christian's Love for the Unseen Christ*, Thomas Vincent wrote:

> This discovery of Christ dispels clouds from the mind, and exhales lusts from the heart. It brightens the understanding and cleanses the affections. It warms the heart with love and fills the heart with comfort; it quiets the conscience and purifies it. It gives a most sweet peace and tranquility to the spirit and, withal, brings in such spiritual joy as is unspeakable and full of glory. O how, then, should you admire the riches of the grace and

kindness of the Lord Jesus Christ unto you! That He should give unto you this manifestation of Himself; when the manifestation is so admirable, so desirable, so useful, and which lifts you up into a far higher degree of excellence than the most accomplished persons in the world that are without this revelation![1]

I love Vincent's words. Discovering Christ clears the mind and purifies the heart. In Jesus we find the most admirable object of the affections.

Are you willing to look for Jesus in the Scriptures? Because He's willing to be found there. You will only make the effort to uneclipse Jesus if you are convinced that the Son behind the eclipse is worth the effort. And friends, only the Bible will convince you of that.

BUT, ONE DAY!

Seeing Jesus by faith is for this world. Seeing Jesus with sight is for the next. We might be tempted to think that if God would show us Himself, we would be better off. Maybe the world would be convinced of His reality and identity. But this is sadly not true.

God did show Himself in flesh and blood for three decades in Israel—in Jesus. But seeing wasn't convincing for the vast majority. Many thought that if Jesus did more miracles people would believe, but three years of wonders and words spoken as no other man ever uttered settled the issue. Most were unmoved. Jesus' life and ministry were accomplished, by and large, behind an eclipse of disbelief and unbelief. If the sight of Jesus and His physical presence did not turn the tide, leaving us a video would do even less. In His infinite wisdom God left us a book, a verbal revelation of Himself to feed and excite our faith.

Yet there will be a day when Moses' prayer to *see* God's glory will be answered, both for him and us. Paul described this to the Corinthian believers when he wrote: "Therefore, being always of good courage, and knowing that while we are at home in the body we are absent from the Lord—for we walk by faith, not by sight—we are of good courage, I say, and prefer rather to be absent from the body and to be at home with the Lord" (2 Corinthians 5:6–8).

In this world we walk by faith with Jesus. But there will be a day when we walk by sight. Read the fourth and fifth chapters of the book of Revelation. Heaven will excite and paralyze the spiritual retina of the redeemed. When sight is added to our faith on that great day, God's revelation of Himself will be overwhelming. Sounds and color and smells and tastes and the touch of our Savior—every sense God created in His people will be alive to the Son, uneclipsed and fully enjoyed.

The heart of faith beats with a longing and wistful anticipation of that day. We will be like Him; we will see Him as He truly is in undiminished glory. When the apostle John was with Jesus before the ascension, he loved Him and worshipped Him. But when He encountered the Son of God in the heavenly vision on the isle of Patmos, he responded with an entirely different perspective. Seeing with sight instead of faith was consequential. "When I *saw* Him, I fell at His feet like a dead man" (Revelation 1:17).

Believers will one day join John at the feet of our Lord. But for now, this hope moves us to obedience and holiness. This same John wrote, "Beloved, now we are children of God, and it has not appeared as yet what we will be. We know that when He appears, we will be like Him, because we will see Him just as He is. And everyone who has this hope fixed on Him purifies himself, just as He is pure" (1 John 3:2–3). This pursuit of purity is the subject of our next chapter.

7

SATAN'S ASSOCIATES

This book is impossible.

The words by which we know God, the Bible, also tell us this: The Son cannot be completely uneclipsed in this life. It's not because He does not wish to reveal Himself to us. And it's not because we don't ache to see Him and know Him as He is in fullness and constancy. It's because there are some things we want more than the all-precious Son of God.

Does that frustrate you? That frustration might be a signal that you're ready. A sign of life. You have that hankering, the "hunger and thirst for righteousness" that alone can satisfy you (Matthew 5:6). Until you begin to face off with the great enemies—within and without—that conspire to obscure the glory of the Son, you will remain asleep in the shadows.

Paul tells the Ephesians in chapter 5 that they were once in the darkness, "but now [they] are Light in the Lord" so they must "walk as children of Light" (v. 8). If you are familiar with this practical portion of the book of Ephesians, you understand that this is a fairly straightforward command to walk in obedience as a child of God through Christ. But in verse 14, Paul reemphasizes the need for believers to be alerted, awakened, invigorated to obedience, and He appends to this command a promise: "For this reason it says, 'Awake, sleeper, and arise from the dead, and Christ will shine on you.'" Though we have hope for the physical resurrection from the dead, here Paul is talking about resurrection from spiritual death. The apostle is saying, *Arise from spiritual slumber! You are light in the Lord; act like it! When you do that, Christ with shine on you.*

Those who feel the pang of daily frustration with their own twilight-walking and heed this command are those whom Christ will especially enlighten! Remember John 14:21 says that if you obey and love Jesus, He will disclose Himself to you. But this awakening—or uneclipsing, as we have called it—isn't easy.

LABOR TO KNOW

We must labor to remove whatever eclipses the glory of Jesus Christ. To do that we must understand biblically the forces arrayed against us. Martin Luther, who faced unimaginable opposition during the Reformation, wrote these famous words of hymnody: "For still our ancient foe doth seek to work us woe; his craft and power are great, and, armed with cruel hate, on earth is not his equal." We know that Satan has blinded the eyes of the lost (2 Corinthians 4:4), but what can Satan do to us? Are his "craft and power" really that great? What does Satan do to distract us? He can't change our minds; He can't force us to do anything. So how does he "work us woe"?

Another great man of the Word, John Owen, takes us a step closer to understanding this concept. He wrote, "Labor to know your own frame and temper; what spirit you are of; what associates in your heart Satan has; where corruption is strong, where grace is weak; what stronghold lust has in your natural constitution, and the like." In other words, know what you're like. Where are your strengths? Where are your weaknesses? When are you inclined to sadness and melancholy? What gets you up? What gets you down? What kind of temperament has God given you? Then Owen asks, "What associates in your heart [does] Satan [have]; where corruption is strong, where grace is weak; what stronghold [does] lust [have] in your natural constitution, and the like?"[1]

Consider the implications of this: Satan has associates in your heart. While he can't make you sin, he can put temptations in your path (2 Corinthians 11:3). Let me use a crude analogy most everyone is familiar with. It seems I'm always trying to lose a few pounds. Now Satan cannot make me eat chocolate soufflé—rich flourless cake, infused with dark, molten chocolate, dressed in chocolate syrup with vanilla ice cream. Satan can put that on the table before me, but he can't make me eat it. But it is just the kind of concoction the devil is likely to put in my heart. He would not, on the other hand, put mushroom soufflé before me because he knows it has no appeal (I hate mushrooms!). Satan has been alive for a long time. His minions have been active and mobilized since the week the world was created. The Scriptures don't give us any indication that they sleep. They're watching you all the time. They recognize your habits and weaknesses, perhaps better than you do. The enemy knows what to put on the table to tempt you.

I was recently asked a very insightful series of questions. Why are some people tempted with adultery, while others aren't? Why are some tempted in homosexuality, while others aren't? Why are some tempted more on the Internet, while some not? Why are some tempted toward gluttony, while some aren't? The truth is we must labor to understand our unique weaknesses, so that we can be prepared for Satan's customized temptations. Do you know where you're weak, where you're strong, what "frame and temper you are of"? Can you identify "the sin which so easily entangles" *you?* (Hebrews 12:1). Do you know what associates Satan has in your heart to lead you toward temptation?

Satan's strategy is the same as it's always been; he disguises himself. He comes as "an angel of light" (2 Corinthians 11:13–15). He's tempting you to do what seems so perfectly fitting for you to engage in. He distracts; he puts the attention on yourself rather than on Christ. He distorts your understanding of the Scriptures, taking the edge off the hard commands of Christ. So it falls to us to study the Scriptures, as we have talked about already, and to study ourselves in the light of them.

A WAR OF ABSTAINING

All this talk about study can make this whole matter of dealing with sin seem a little…academic. But it's not. The truth is, you are in a war.

First Peter 2 describes this war. You are held captive by a real and determined enemy; you are engaged in a fight with that enemy. But here's the catch: *You* are that enemy. Peter writes in verse 11, "Beloved, I urge you as aliens and strangers to abstain from fleshly lusts which wage war against the soul." While Satan has a hand in serving up temptations to sin, the real war is waged within your own soul. The war is inside. Your fleshly desires and lusts wage war against the soul within you that wants to be pure and sanctified and holy, standing in the blazing and unobstructed light of the Son.

The word "abstain" carries the sense of "holding yourself back from" your sinful desires, having self-discipline. The phrase "fleshly lusts" describes those desires which are natural to you. Galatians 5:17 says that "the flesh sets its desire against the Spirit, and the Spirit against the flesh; for these are in opposition to one another, so that you may not do the things that you please." What audacity you have in your sinful, native desires that you make war on the very Spirit of God who sealed you in union with Christ and has given you spiritual life!

You're in a serious battle. The question is, are you awake? Are you alerted to the enemies you face? If you claim to know the Savior and you know nothing of this battle, you're in serious trouble. Do you find yourself identifying and hating particular sins? Have you gone beyond merely being annoyed by those sins? Does the alarm of your conscience actually work, or have you hit the snooze button so many times you just ignore it? Are there virtues in Christ you desire that seem out of your reach? Do you see evidences of the fruit of the Spirit in your life? Are you bothered by the fruit of the flesh that's in your life?

If you're in that battle and you hate it, take heart. I love what John Piper says: "If you are fighting sin, you are alive. Take heart. But if sin holds sway unopposed, you are dead no matter how lively this sin makes you feel. Take heart, embattled saint!"[2] The temporary titillation of some indulged sin is the vestige of an old life, the phantom pains of a limb that has long since been amputated, the flicker of an extinguished star. Take heart! Dig in! Hold the line!

John Owen wrote famously, "Be killing sin or it will be killing you." I've killed a few snakes in my life. There are very few of them that die with one whack. You have snakes that are crawling in your soul. They grow new heads every day. It's not a one-time battle. This eclipse that's blocking the Son comes from within you. Satan knows what your temptations are. These associates in your heart make you inclined to certain sins, and just understanding these entrenched realities is tremendously important if you would move toward the perfect light of the Son.

Owen continues, "There are two great things that are suitable to humble the souls of men. The first is a due consideration of God. And the second is a due consideration of yourself. Of God, look at His greatness, His glory, His holiness, His power, His majesty and His authority, and of ourselves, to understand our mean, lowly, insignificant abject sinful condition."[3] Are you an expert on where the enemy is most likely to tempt you? Do you understand the character of God and do you understand your own character? When you do, you will agree with J. C. Ryle who said, "Terribly black must be that guilt for which nothing but the blood of the Son of God could make satisfaction."[4]

IDOLS ALL

So you understand your problem is sin.

And your sin is not the result of a bad childhood, of insufficient training, of some traumatic event, of the negative influence of others in your life, of the media, of the society you live in, nor of your low self esteem, or even of the devil himself. No, God killed His Son for how bad *you* are (Isaiah 53:10). He sacrificed His only begotten boy for the vileness of your own heart. As Jesus taught us, "'For from within, out of the heart of men, proceed the evil thoughts, fornications, thefts, murders, adulteries, deeds of coveting and wickedness, as well as deceit, sensuality, envy, slander, pride and foolishness. All these evil things proceed from within and defile the man'" (Mark 7:21–23). And against these evil desires in ourselves we have squared off in mortal combat.

But we come next to the question perhaps most critical to the success of our campaign. What is sin, really?

Paul answers that question in Colossians 3:5, writing, "Consider the members of your earthly body as dead to immorality, impurity, passion, evil desire, and greed, which amounts to idolatry." Paul wraps up all sinning in a single descriptor that is…unsettling. And it should be.

Immorality,

impurity,

passion,

evil desire,

and greed,

which amounts to *idolatry.* We should be dead to all this. Carrying on this old life is a kind of wrongful worship. And that's the essence of sin.

Idols have come between you and the Son of God, eclipsing His glory in your life.

In 1 Corinthians 8–10, Paul addresses Christian liberties, pleasures, things we can rightfully enjoy. But others have "issues" with some of these things. And Paul essentially instructs the Corinthians, *Don't sacrifice the effectiveness of your ministry to others just for things you enjoy.* It's a rich and practical passage, but at the end, as he did in Colossians, Paul gives them one final directive in this matter, He says in 14:10, "Therefore, my beloved, flee from idolatry." Enjoying something good at the expense of another's conscience is worshipping that something more than Christ, who would have you lovingly consider them. Again, anything you indulge in that contradicts the obedient worship of Christ is a wrongful worship. You've made yourself an idol, a substitute that shades you from Christ's glory.

And Paul's not alone on the record here. John also speaks to it in yet another surprising turn to the subject of idolatry. The epistle of 1 John ends with perhaps the greatest affirmation of the deity of Christ in the New Testament. First John 5:20–21 reads, "And we know that the Son of God has come, and has given us understanding so that we may know Him who is true; and we are in Him who is true, in His Son Jesus

Christ. This is the true God and eternal life." It's pretty clear, is it not? He is ending on a high theological note. But then the elder John in his exhortative, practical wisdom gives one final fatherly instruction: "Little children, guard yourselves from idols." As if to say, *Little ones, you have the true One; worship Him alone. That's the main thing.*

Idolatry is the worship of anything or anyone other than *Him*.

I love Jonah's description of idols. His insight is penetrating. Jonah 2:8 says, "Those who regard vain idols forsake their faithfulness." But the term *vain idols* there literally means "false vanities." The word for "idol" is the same word used in Ecclesiastes for "vanity." An idol is a lying, temporary experience, a false vanity telling you that a temporary, fleeting pleasure will satisfy you, last just as long as you need it to, and give you just precisely what you want. That's what idols do.

Now we understand how people make idols out of relationships.

"I want this boyfriend."

"I want this girlfriend."

"I want this husband."

"I want this wife."

"I want these children because they will give me what I want."

Others make idols out of material possessions.

"I want this car because this car is going to give me what I want, to be looked up to, noticed."

And the moment we are willing to sin to obtain or maintain these things, they have become our idols. Substitutes for the living God. These perfectly good things have become in our lives and hearts no different than other sins, such as those Paul compiled in Ephesians: immorality, impurity, passion, evil desire, and greed. We think we know what we want. We think we know what we need. But God gives us all we need in Himself. This is the essence of Jonathan Edwards's theology: *God is not only in it for Himself. He gives us Himself, and that's the best thing He can give us.*

There are idols in your heart from which you must "flee," "guard yourself," and "awaken" such that "Christ will shine on you." You have to identify them, see them for what they are, and turn again to worship the "true One" alone. You can no longer give your attentions to these things if you would uneclipse the Son of God.

STOPPING WITHOUT STARTING

What will wake us up from these empty dreams, the lying vanities that suffocate our love for Christ and shade our eyes from His glory?

I've counseled countless people in decades of ministry, yet I have never come to a counseling session where someone said, "I'm struggling with this sin and it's killing me, and I'm also learning so much about Jesus that my quiet times have never been better!" It's never happened, and I suspect it never will.

"Could it be," I ask them, "that Jesus is *a part* of your life and not *the point* of your life? Could it be? You're wondering, *Why am I struggling?* Could it be that you're simply trying to *stop* sinning without really ever *starting* to simply worship Jesus?"

The Galatian believers also needed to understand the fullness of this equation, so Paul made it very plain in his letter to them, in Galatians 5:16–17: "But I say, walk by the Spirit and you will not carry out the desire of the flesh. For the flesh sets its desire against the Spirit, and the Spirit against the flesh; for these are in opposition to one another, so that you may not do the things that you please." The next six verses describe the deeds of the flesh and the fruit of the Spirit, but understand that these lists are fruit, consequences, effects. The natural condition of our souls produces and enjoys the desires of the flesh. But when we walk in step with the Spirit of God, the character of Jesus is produced in us.

There is a critical clue in plain sight for how this works. It is in verse 24: "Now those who belong to Christ Jesus have crucified the flesh with its passions and desires." It is Jesus' ownership of our lives that flexes the soul's muscles to fight against the flesh. Fighting sin is not the stuff of will power; it is the result of Jesus' power, uneclipsed.

Only Jesus can do that, but it does involve our energies. We must "put on the Lord Jesus Christ, and make no provision for the flesh in regard to its lusts" (Romans 13:14). Now we're starting to see more clearly how Jesus uneclipses Himself for us. You have to put Him on. He has to be more beautiful, more satisfying, more precious than what's between you and Him. The Greek word translated "provision" can be translated "strategy" or "forethought." If we are not thinking ahead and strategizing about how our lives will align with Christ and His pleasures, we will surely indulge in fleshly gratification. There is no middle ground.

PUTTING AWAY CHILDISH THINGS

Those who "belong to Jesus" as Paul describes are moving toward Him on a course of maturation. As you grow in the knowledge of Christ and set about "killing sin" in your life, you're growing up as a believer. It's important to understand how this works. First Corinthians 13:11 talks about this process: "When I was a child, I used to speak like a child, think like a child, reason like a child; when I became a man, I did away with childish things." A mature believer is always putting away those sins that entangle him.

We are not alone in the process. God's design is to have parents help their children grow up. My wife and I are constantly trying to aid our three sons as they make progress in their maturity. Keeping them focused and on task is a never-ending duty. Spiritual maturity is no different. That is why God designed spiritual leadership in the fellowship of the church. We'll look at this more closely in the next chapter, but it suffices to say that gifted men have been given to the church to equip us for spiritual service and to build up the body of Christ, the church. Paul describes this in Ephesians 4:11–15:

And He gave some *as* apostles, and some *as* prophets, and some *as* evangelists, and some *as* pastors and teachers, for the equipping of the saints for the work of service, to the building up of the body of Christ; until we all attain to the unity of the faith, and of the knowledge of the Son of God, to a mature man, to the measure of the stature which belongs to the fullness of Christ. As a result, we are no longer to be children, tossed here and there by waves and carried about by every wind of doctrine, by the trickery of men, by craftiness in deceitful scheming; but speaking the truth in love, we are to grow up in all *aspects* into Him who is the head, *even* Christ.

The goal of everything we do in church is contained in that rich phrase in verse 13: "the knowledge of the Son of God, to a mature man, to the measure of the stature which belongs to the fullness of Christ." Your spiritual maturity is based on your knowledge and understanding of who Jesus is and what He did.

Oh, but it gets even more glorious as you keep going in this passage. The knowledge of Jesus results in doctrinal stability and spiritual equilibrium, and this means we are "to grow up in all aspects into Him who is the head, even Christ" (v. 15). Jesus is the target! He is the means by which we grow, and He is the destination of our growth.

Notice that this growth is comprehensive. It involves "all aspects"— work, play, school, responsibilities, relationships, morning, noon, night—every dimension and every category of life. Maturity is growth by Him, through Him, to Him. Again, this progress is at the same time toward Christ and away from sin. Jesus and sin are 180 degrees from each other. It is impossible to move toward Jesus and sin simultaneously.

Those who live for the sinful desires of the flesh are described in verses 17–19:

> "So this I say, and affirm together with the Lord, that you walk no longer just as the Gentiles also walk, in the futility of their mind, being darkened in their understanding, excluded from the life of God because of the ignorance that is in them, because of the hardness of their heart; and they, having become callous, have given themselves over to sensuality for the practice of every kind of impurity with greediness."

What a bleak picture: darkened understanding, exclusion from God's life, ignorance, hard heartedness, and practicing every kind of impurity. This is life for the unbeliever. You might expect the apostle to contrast this hellishness with the life of a believer by saying something like, "You have learned to live differently," or "This is not reflective of the doctrine I taught you." But listen to how the Christian life is described: "But you did not learn Christ in this way" (v. 20). How do you learn how to walk differently from the world? How do you learn to fight the indwelling sin from which you've been saved?

You learn Christ.

Please, please, please don't miss this: holiness, growth, and maturity in your Christian walk is enlarging, expanding, intensifying, escalating, increasing, and clarifying your understanding of Jesus. If you want to learn how to please the Lord, if you really want to move the eclipse out of the way, you must learn Christ.

THOU, MY BEST THOUGHT

Eleanor Hull's 1912 versification of the old Irish Hymn "Be Thou My Vision" articulates what it means to learn Christ. The first verse contains the familiar line, "Thou my best thought by day or by night." Add to that the later line, "Thou and Thou only first in my heart, high King of heaven, my treasure Thou art." These lines describe an unspeakably powerful weapon for winning the fight against sin. I think it is the most powerful of all sanctifying graces. It is to sin what the nuclear warhead is to battle. This weapon is called appraisal.

As I write this chapter we are in the process of selling our home. There are countless elements that go into both buying and selling a house. If you have never bought or sold a house, don't be shocked by the stack of papers you have to sign as you close the deal. If you have been through this process before, you know what I mean.

Of all the parts of making a home purchase, the most important is the appraisal. Everything depends on it. The appraisal is the process of assessing the home's value. It tells you what it is worth. Once you see what the home's value is, you decide if that value is worth the price.

Listen to the indicators of our hymn's appraisal of Jesus—"my *best* thought," "*first* in my heart," "my *treasure* Thou art." These words reveal a deliberate evaluation of Jesus' worth, a comparison of His value to everything else. And when our Savior and His good news are measured against any pleasure and certainly any sin, the contrast is astonishing. Spiritual health is determined by the frequency and depth of our thoughts of Jesus.

Sin eclipses the Son. And only the thought of Jesus can cause the eclipse to recede.

If you are going to fight in the war against your sin, you will need to arm yourself with a thoroughly biblical and powerful appraisal of the Son.

The context for appropriate evaluation of the Savior is the gospel. Peter's last word, his last safeguard, his final testament was simply this: "Grow in the grace and knowledge of our Lord and Savior Jesus Christ" (2 Peter 3:18). To mature in grace is to better understand the depth and breadth of our sin and the unspeakably precious death of the Son of God to atone for it. To grow in the knowledge of Jesus is to compare Him to everything and see His superiority. "For to me, to live is Christ and to die is gain" (Philippians 1:21). As Paul measures life and death, heaven and earth, Jesus is his best thought.

The gospel is more than a plan; it is the person of Jesus. And the gospel is priceless.

In Matthew 13 Jesus told several parables, including two that speak directly to this. They only take a few seconds to read, but they take a lifetime to apply. You probably know them well: "The kingdom of heaven is like a treasure hidden in the field, which a man found and hid *again;* and from joy over it he goes and sells all that he has and buys that field. Again, the kingdom of heaven is like a merchant seeking fine pearls, and upon finding one pearl of great value, he went and sold all that he had and bought it" (Matthew 13:44–46). The point is obvious. The gospel, which *is* Jesus, is the treasure and the pearl worthy of any sacrifice, any price, every effort. Is He really that valuable?

In two staccato questions our Lord asked His disciples to answer the ultimate issue of the value of worldly pleasures, vain pursuits, and deceitful sins. He asked, "For what will it profit a man if he gains the whole world and forfeits his soul? Or what will a man give in exchange for his soul?" (Matthew 16:26). How about you? Is there anything that you will give in exchange for your soul?

So what do we do with this world? How should we evaluate the temptations it offers? Martin Luther offers this sound counsel:

> Conduct yourselves as those who are no longer citizens of the world, for your possessions lie not on this earth but in heaven; and although you may have lost all temporal goods, you still have Christ, who is more than all else. The devil is the prince of this world and rules it. His citizens are the people of the world. Therefore since you are not of the world, act as a stranger in an inn, who does not have his possessions with him but merely procures food and spends his money for it. For this world is merely a place of transit, where we cannot stay; we must travel farther. Therefore we should use worldly goods only to shelter and sustain ourselves before we depart and go to another land. In heaven we are citizens; on earth we are pilgrims and guests.[5]

Does Satan have associates in your heart that whisper, or perhaps yell, into the ear of your soul that the pleasures of this world and its lusts of deceit (Ephesians 4:22) will make you happy, better, satisfied?

If I could boil everything I've said down into one sentence, I would borrow the words of William Featherston in 1864. You've probably sung it dozens and dozens of times. Will you sing it again with prayerful affection for Jesus?

"My Jesus, I love Thee. I know Thou art mine."

For Thee all the follies of sin I resign."

8

JESUS, MARRIED?

Standing outside the lunchroom in high school one day, I heard a theory that still tilts my head. A young lady informed me that there was a lot more to Jesus than what I had in my Bible. I had no problem with this part. John even says at the end of his gospel that if all the things that could be written about Jesus were written, all of the books in the world could not contain them (John 21:25). But what she proceeded to explain about Jesus of Nazareth, I want to confess, shook me up a bit.

"You know He had girlfriends," she said, "and was probably even married."

Somehow, I thought, *in writing four Gospels and spending all that time with the Lord, the disciples strangely omitted this detail in their record of Him.*

Of course it isn't true. Jesus was not married. Gnostic teachers, however, popularized these myths in the centuries following His ascension. We find no credible source, no credible reference or record that He ever had any romantic attachments, much less a girlfriend, a mistress, or a wife. But while we may be quick to relegate such ideas to the realm of pop theology, we do well to stop and consider the claims the Bible does make in this regard from the book of Revelation.

Revelation 19:7 says, "Let us rejoice and be glad and give glory to Him, for the marriage of the Lamb has come and His bride has made herself ready." Two chapters later John continues this amazing theme: "Then one of the seven angels who had the seven bowls full of the seven last plagues came and spoke with me, saying, 'Come here, I will show you the bride, the wife of the Lamb'" (Revelation 21:9; see also Isaiah 54:5-6).

Wait a minute, *the wife of the Lamb?*

The truth is, while Jesus is not nor ever has been married, He's going to be. In fact, He's already engaged. Jesus Christ has chosen a bride. He is betrothed to her and He does not break His word. In Ephesians 5:22–33, Paul takes this profound analogy even further in his explanation of the dynamics of marriage. A husband is supposed to lovingly lead his wife while the wife is to joyfully submit to her husband, mirroring Christ and His bride, who is none other than the church (not Mary Magdalene).

THE CHURCH'S ONE FOUNDATION

The concept may seem basic, but the longer I'm a Christian and the longer I'm a pastor, the more confusion I see in practice and hear in popular Christian teaching about the church. Who talks about the church being the bride, the betrothed of Christ with whom He's united through His own death and resurrection in a spiritual love relationship? If you find yourself in a discussion about the church with the emerging generation, you almost always hear certain buzz words. If the conversation gets a little bit critical, evaluating a certain church, you'll typically hear hip-sounding terms that circle around the words *community*, *authenticity*, and everyone's favorite, *relevance*. There's talk about chipping in on social issues, about everyone finding their *purpose*.

Now don't get me wrong; some of those words are good words and some of those concepts are really good ones. Some of them are a part of the connective tissue described in the Bible regarding the identity of church. Unfortunately, they are most often used in a manner that sidelines the church's real purpose and commission. We're witnessing an entire generation trying to reinvent the church, trying to solve a problem that doesn't really exist. I read a book recently in which the author's basic premise is: "Everything you've thought about the church is wrong, and what I have to say about the church is now the right way to do it." The problem is that people tend to evaluate the church by their own personal experience with the church; it's a horizontal kind of evaluation and relationship. Their thinking boils down to:

Church is about me, community, us, how we're dealing with each other, what we're doing in the world and with the world.

While those are facets of church ministry, if you read the New Testament you find the church is defined more by Jesus than it is by us and our relationships. The church says together,

Let us rejoice and be glad and give glory to Him!

Perhaps many who are discontent with the church simply haven't found contentment in Jesus. Every church you are ever going to be involved with is going to, at some level, in some way, eventually disappoint you. The pastor will say something you don't like, the deacons and elders will make decisions you're not in tune with, and you're going to find yourself saying, internally and intuitively, *I want to quit this church and go find a better church that's more in line with my idea about church.*

Now, leaving a church isn't always bad. Sometimes it's a good and noble decision. My question is, in which church are you going to find that perfect fit? I know where it is: heaven. What many of these trendy teachings about the church fail to recognize is the true identity and biblical purpose of the church. Church is not a support group for life. The church is not about us finding each other and connecting with each other. These may be wonderful benefits of our fellowship, but only if they are a result of being attached to our Head, our Bridegroom, the Lord Jesus Christ. Sadly, the knee-jerk reaction in most of our conversations about church is to focus on ourselves and our relationships with one another *before* and maybe even *to the exclusion of* our talk about Christ. Now understand, these are extremely important relationships. However, they're not supremely important. What's supremely important is the church's relationship with Jesus. We are His bride. He is our Head.

LAB COATS IN THE DESERT

Some of you may be old enough to remember the nuclear test movies made for public awareness during the Cold War. Scores of scientists wearing lab coats and thick sunglasses assembled in the desert to watch a nuclear detonation at a safe distance. The intense brightness of the fission reaction was the subject of their total attention. It was their study and their obsession. So it is with the church, gathered to gaze upon the blazing glory of the Son, Jesus Christ. Not consumed with man-centered ideologies and trendy theologyspeak, but endeavoring together to uneclipse the Son and to "know Him and the power of His resurrection" (Philippians 3:10).

Jesus is the point and focus of the church. *Church* is a small word, coming from a big Greek word, *ekklesia*, which simply means a gathering of people, a group. Even the word *Ecclesiastes* in the Old Testament just meant a group of people that Solomon was preaching to. If you're serious about uneclipsing Jesus, you're going to need some help from friends. And those friends are the church, a group of people echoing back to their Lord and Master and Savior His glories, saying together, "Behold the Lamb!"

It is critical to our understanding of the church that we move from a primarily horizontal orientation to a vertical orientation. To this end I want to provide some key principles for getting church right. If you can get these principles down, you're going to save yourself a world of discontentment throughout your Christian life as you select churches, and as you observe the inevitable imperfections of churches and church leaders.

I WILL BUILD IT

The church belongs to Jesus.

Matthew 16 contains the first instance of the word *church* in the New Testament. It is used by Christ in a conspicuous and yet wonderful way. As He is travelling in Caesarea Philippi, He pulls His disciples aside to talk to them. Keep in mind that Jesus has been teaching and healing and multiplying food and walking on water. He has been doing all sorts of miraculous things in the Galilean area, and people are starting to talk.

Who is this guy? Where's He from? What's He about?

Jesus knows the rumor mill is in full swing, so He pulls His men aside and asks them, "Who do people say that the Son of Man is?" (Matthew 16:13).

This gives us some insight into the disciples' relationship with Jesus. They weren't with Him 24/7, but because they were a part of the Lord's entourage, as they moved about and interacted with people they had no doubt many discussions about their Master, the miracle worker. Jesus is asking the disciples to update Him about the rumors. What are people saying? In verse 14, the disciples let Him in on the gossip…

Well, some say You're John the Baptist. Now that is more than a bit strange, even spooky. John the Baptist was beheaded a few months earlier. How could they think He's John the Baptist if He and John the Baptist were alive at the same time and were seen together?

Others say You're Elijah. This is more biblical at least. They associated Jesus with that great prophet who did so many miraculous things.

Still others say Jeremiah. Jeremiah was a great prophet and a great teacher.

Or one of the prophets. Maybe He's Hosea, Amos, Obadiah? Who knows?

Finally Jesus turns the question toward them in verse 15: *Hey, one more question. Who do you say that I am?*

This is a pop quiz, a pass-fail test of epic proportions. Two and a half years they've been with Jesus, and now He puts it to them. What are they going to say? True to form, the disciple with the foot-shaped mouth speaks first in verse 16: "Simon Peter answered, 'You are the Christ, the Son of the living God.'" A remarkable, even miraculous response, all the more so because Jesus had originally asked, "Who do people say the *Son of Man* is?" Peter answers, "You're the Son of God," demonstrating his grasp of the incarnation.

Jesus said to him, "Blessed are you, Simon Barjona" (v. 17). Peter must have glowed. You can just see him elbowing the other disciples. *I got it right!* But Jesus takes the opportunity to expand on an unexpected theme. He says "I also say to you that you are Peter, and upon this rock I will build My church; and the gates of Hades will not overpower it" (v. 18). The rock of Peter's confession of the character of Jesus Christ would become the foundation of the church, "and the gates of Hades will not overpower it." That's an amazing, jaw-dropping affirmation in itself. The Son of God and Man was going to break ground on something new, declaring with resolve: "I will build My church."

Jesus is building the church. Not just the church, *His* church. The church belongs to Jesus. Don't miss the fact that this first description of the church is in the context of the identity of Jesus as the Messiah. If you're a disciple affirming Jesus is the Messiah, in the same stroke you affirm that He's going to build His church.

Our Lord clearly declares ownership, calling it, "My church," and the history of the church is a history of the success and persistence of Christ's people against a world that is like the gates of Hades, wanting to topple it. In Colossians 1:18 Paul writes, "He is also head of the body, the church; and He is the beginning, the firstborn from the dead, so that He Himself will come to have first place in everything." The church belongs to Jesus, as does all else. We say somewhat casually, "This is my church" or "This is our church." We all know what we mean by this, but how important it is for us to reckon that ultimately it's Christ's church. And the sooner we recognize that this gathering belongs to Jesus, the more clearly we bring Him in His radiant glory into focus and set aside our own perceived "needs" and expectations.

BUILT INTO CHRIST

The church is Christ's and He will build it...for Himself.

Paul's book of Ephesians is one of the primary sources of our understanding of the rich theology of the church. What is the church for? Why does it exist? Ephesians1:22–23 reads, "And He put all things in subjection under His feet, and gave Him as head over all things to the church, which is His body, the fullness of Him who fills all in all." Remarkably, Paul doesn't stop at saying Jesus is the head of the church; he makes it clear that Jesus is the head of all creation. God gave the head of all creation to the church as its head. We didn't just get some angel. We didn't get one of the archangels. We got the head of creation, God Himself, in flesh, Jesus Christ. He's the head of our assembly.

As we saw in the last chapter from Ephesians 4, believers are unified in the church for the privileged purpose of coming to a deeper knowledge of the Son of God (vv. 11–13). Things work horizontally in the church *when* we enjoy and respond to knowing the Son of God. When believers understand, know, and are still actively pursuing a knowledge of the uneclipsed Jesus, then we see the church as all He saved her for, built her to be, and commissioned her to do. The result is described at the end of Paul's tremendous run-on sentence: we become "...a mature man, to the measure of the stature which belongs to the fullness of Christ. As a result, we are no longer to be children, tossed here and there by waves and carried about by every wind of doctrine" (vv. 13–14).

No longer bowled over by what everyone says about God or the church or Jesus, by the waves of trendsetter theologies, "...by the trickery of men, by craftiness in deceitful scheming; but speaking the truth in love, we are to grow up in all aspects into Him who is the head, even Christ, from whom the whole body, being fitted and held together by what every joint supplies, according to the proper working of each individual part, causes the growth of the body for the building up of itself in love" (vv.14–16).

Let me summarize all of that. The goal of our gathering is to come to maturity in Christ. The goal of our relationships is to encourage and spur one another on to maturity in Christ. The church exists for Jesus, for maturity in Jesus, for knowledge of Jesus, for growth *in* Jesus, for growth *to* Jesus. I think the biggest, most fundamental problem of every human heart saved by grace entering into the church is simply this: we come to the church with the expectation that this is going to be something for us before it is something for Jesus. Make no mistake; the church has incredible blessings to benefit us! But these only come when we are something for Him, a people gathered in love and in adoration, gazing on His unimaginable power and glory in the desert of this world, crying out together, "Let us rejoice and be glad and give glory to Him!"

YOU LEFT ME

We're not far at this juncture from where we began this book. Remember when the messenger brought the letter from Jesus to the little church at Ephesus, a church blessed beyond our imagination's capability to understand?

Put yourself in their sandals for a minute. They're meeting for church, and a messenger knocks on the door. "I've got a letter for you!"

"Really? Who's it from?"

"Jesus."

"Um, we should all hear this letter! Change the bulletin for this morning!"

Jesus came to John in a vision on the isle of Patmos and dictated this message for their hearing (Revelation 2:1–7). Let me paraphrase it like this:

Hey, you've done great! You stand against false teachers, you identify error, and you're doing a lot of great ministry for Me. Great work! The churchgoers are looking pretty satisfied with themselves to this point, feeling so good about this letter from Jesus. And then He says, *But I have this against you: you left your first love—you left Me. And now you've lost Me in the endless escalator of Christian activity. Without Me, you're getting nowhere.* The organ stops.

Reader, the church exists for Jesus. He built it so He would be loved and worshiped in spirit and in truth, not to whip the members into a frenzy of Christianness. Before you're critical of any church, ask yourself if your own heart is more inclined toward Jesus because of your association with these people.

Jesus, Jesus, Jesus is the focus of the gathering of the redeemed in fellowships across the globe and in the realm of heaven beyond it. One of my favorite descriptions of the church is in Philippians 3:3: "For we are the true circumcision, who worship in the Spirit of God and glory in Christ Jesus and put no confidence in the flesh." He's saying that believers are not like those of the Jewish circumcision, a system which does not lead to salvation and is based on works. But rather, the church comprises those who glory in and worship Jesus. Preaching, teaching, music, and fellowship should all direct our attention to the glory of Jesus. The gathering of Christians, called the church, has a signature with three characters: we worship God, glory in Jesus, and don't trust our flesh.

RELEVANT TO JESUS

At this point, you may be saying, *Well, there's a lot of "one anothers" in the Bible. Aren't you deemphasizing those?* My point is that we have nothing to offer each other apart from Jesus. If we are not filled with His Spirit and worshipping Him through His Word, the "one anothers" are fruitless. The church is supposed to be a group of believers helping one another uneclipse the Son, a group of believers helping one another to live for Jesus, to serve Him by serving one another.

Perhaps the most misguided church strategy of our time, maybe of all of church history, is this thing called the "seeker movement," where the idea is to create an environment and a group to try to get unbelievers to come to the church to get saved. Now, don't misunderstand; I believe that unbelievers should come to the church and find the gospel when they do. But the church is not designed for unbelievers. The church is a place where believers are equipped to go out into the world and proclaim the gospel.

God did not design evangelism to be a "herd them up and brand them" operation where we bring all the "seekers" we can to church so the pastor can brand them with the gospel. No, the mission is just the opposite. In fact, Paul writes in Romans 3:10–11, "'There is none righteous, not even one; there is none who understands, there is none who seeks for God." If there are none who seek God, then who are these seekers? I believe in seeker services in which God is the Seeker and He seeks to save and sanctify those who are under the hearing of His Word. We must praise the Lord for people who have been brought to church and have been blessed and saved, but we cannot let the church become an evangelistic meeting place at the expense of it being a place to equip believers. We gather to edify; we scatter to evangelize.

While we are talking about what the church is for, let me address the myth of relevance. I began hearing this term when I was in college: "We need to make the church relevant," built on the assumption that the church in its present state is not relevant. And the question is, relevant to whom and for whom? Just who should the church be relevant for?

The correct answer is, very simply, Jesus.

We're called to be relevant to and for Christ because we're faithful in service and ministry. A century ago, the church wanted to become relevant, that is, relevant in the eyes of the world. So it sought the approval of scholars, of the academy, of the universities, especially those coming out of Germany at the time. Many church leaders of the day appeared to conclude: "They think that we're not intelligent because we believe in miracles, the deity of Christ, that the Bible is a supernatural book inspired by God. The scholars say the supernatural doesn't happen based on the empirical rationalism of the enlightenment. Therefore, the Bible can't be right."

So the church started saying, "If they disrespect us for believing in miracles, we need to find a way around that. The Bible doesn't mean six days. It means six ages. We don't really believe that the Red Sea was parted and the Egyptians were drowned in it. It was the Reed Sea." The church started inventing arguments undermining the supernatural nature of Scripture. And that led to liberalism. Get this: the church wanted to be relevant in the eyes of the world, so it chose to do so by becoming academically credible in the eyes of liberal scholarship.

We find many in the church succumbing to the same temptation today. Imprudent believers in the church still want to be seen as relevant to the world. But instead of trying to impress the academics, they want to impress the culture. So now it's cool to be cool...at church. But do you know who you attract when you're cool? Cool people and people who want to be cool. This is a tried and true principle: whatever you use to draw people in is what you'll have to use to keep them coming. As we described in chapter 2, we want visitors in our fellowships to be in awe of the glories of Christ in the gospel. As the psalmist describes, "He put a new song in my mouth, a song of praise to our God; many will see and fear and will trust in the LORD" (Psalm 40:3), we want guests to fear and trust, along with us, in the Redeemer. The culture is not impressed with us, and the church is not the place to try to impress them. Relevance is a myth. We only need to be relevant to God, orienting ourselves toward Christ's glory.

A PLACE TO LEARN

Learning will help you uneclipse Jesus in your life and fully experience the disclosure that He promises in John 14:21. And part of God's design for the church is that it be a context for learning His Word.

Learning? Really? That doesn't sound very appealing...Don't print that on the visitor pamphlet!

Paul explains this to Timothy in 1 Timothy 3:15: "But in case I am delayed, I write so that you will know how one ought to conduct himself in the household of God, which is the church of the living God, the pillar and support of the truth." I love the two illustrations here. The church is the household of God. There's that very valid and important horizontal element. We're brothers and sisters. But note also the second element: the church is the "pillar and support of the truth." It's possible that Paul had in mind the temple of Diana right in downtown Ephesus, which was adorned by 127 gold-plated pillars that held up the roof. But rather than upholding and supporting pagan goddesses and values, the church of the living God upholds the truth of Scripture.

A postmodern worldview suggests a message of secular salvation with self-improvement and self-gratification through self-empowerment and self-consciousness. But the Bible reveals to us the truth about God, about ourselves, about our sin, about condemnation, about our salvation, redemption, and sanctification, even our glorification. The Bible tells us everything important, and the church is the place where that life-giving content is made available and revered as God's truth. The church, while not the exclusive context for learning biblical principles, is nevertheless made magnificent by faithfully upholding and offering to willing hearers the precious words of God. Paul emphasized this again later in 1 Timothy 4:13: "Until I come, give attention to the public reading of Scripture, to exhortation and teaching."

WORSHIP JESUS BY CARING

It's significant that perhaps the most practical, horizontal, relationship-centered passage in all of Scripture is about the worship of Jesus: Romans 12. Nothing is more practical than worshipping Christ by serving and caring for others. At the heart of the application is verse 10: "Be devoted to one another in brotherly love." Take care of one another. Be devoted to one another by helping each other; by helping each other worship Jesus better. Every relationship in the church ought to have as its goal the movement of each person toward worshipping Jesus better. Any friendship that doesn't move you toward a better relationship with Christ is not a spiritual friendship. Any relationship with the opposite sex that's not moving you toward a higher worship of Jesus, toward greater involvement in the church, is taking you away from Him. Acts 2 pictures a people who cared for each other. If somebody had a need, they met it. They didn't just give to the church and expect that to cover it. They cared for each other. Do you know what you have to do to care for one another? You have to know enough about each other to know how to care. You have to know enough about Christ to share Him. Caring is essential to worship; worship always involves caring.

A WAR FOR SIMPLE WORSHIP

My cousin Teri was born with cerebral palsy.

Her story and her struggles marked my life. She had complications in her birth and was born with the crippling disease. Some of my favorite memories are of caring for Teri. She experienced life so differently from me. She couldn't walk, couldn't talk. She could only communicate by certain gestures with her eyes.

While her body was racked by the disease, her mind was fully there. You could ask her questions and she'd respond intelligently by moving her eyes. *Yes* was up and *no* was squeezing her eyes tightly shut.

In God's sweet grace and mercy she received Christ by simply looking up when her parents gave her the gospel. There's something profound in that...

One of the many difficulties Teri faced was terrible, spasmodic attacks where her body would lose control. We would put socks on her hands so she wouldn't scratch her face. She just wasn't able to control it. Sometimes she would hurt herself. These fits were difficult to watch. She was at war with herself, in spite of her own intentions.

When she was twelve she contracted pneumonia. A few days later she laid aside her broken body and went to be with Jesus. I often wonder at the simplicity of her life and how sweet heaven must have been when her faith became sight.

Years later as I was studying the church in 1 Corinthians 12, a light switched on. Paul carefully describes the church with the metaphor of the human body. It's a gripping analogy. In the body, Jesus is the head, and we're its members, the body parts. Paul says, *You know, there's some showy members, and some unseemly members.* There are members that you can see: hands, faces, knees, legs, and arms. Then there are the hidden members: organs, brains, sinuses. You need all of them for the body to function rightly.

So he says, *If you have up-front gifts, great, and if you have behind-the-scenes gifts, great.* But they all have the same purpose of moving the body to love and worship Jesus and serve one another better. Are you aware of your part in the body of Christ, not just to participate in making church better, but to participate in helping the people around you know and love Jesus better? Again 2 Peter 3:18 charges, "Grow in the grace and knowledge of our Lord and Savior Jesus Christ." How do we help each other do that? By loving and using our gifts in His body.

Sometimes the church acts like my cousin. Jesus is the head, sending out signals and relaying instructions, saying, "Work together for Me," and then the parts of the body fight each other, scratching and clawing. Read the book of Philippians, where Paul just says, *Come on, you guys; you can have better unity than this.* Our unity bonds us so that we're growing together into maturity into the fullness of Christ. "Church" is a group of people getting together as often as possible and relating to one another, under the structure that Scripture defines, so that we can uneclipse the Son with and for one another. And if you don't know Jesus, you're not a part of that group.

There's a great temptation for Christians to attempt to transform the precious bride of Jesus into something else: a theater for the arts, a protest movement, a political movement, a social club, even a singles bar. And I daresay it's a temptation for many of us to transform the church into a social construct to be evaluated and criticized, rather than a body in which we participate and serve and, all-importantly, worship the Son.

9

THE LOST SUPPER

Everyone loves a helpful tip, some secret insight.

Investors are always looking for a word on a promising corner of the market. Athletes love to get a hold of a new training technique to gain a performance advantage. Cooks are on the lookout for a new recipe, a secret ingredient, or a new temperature at which to prepare their food. Every student wants pointers on teachers and courses to avoid or add.

Christians are the same way, endlessly seeking out the new and improved "angle" on the Christian life. What trendsetting book, sermon series, conference, or spiritual discipline plan can help us feel vital and growing? How can we sustain the momentum of faith? There's got to be something we're missing. If you're honest, you'll admit that deep inside you're hoping to discover a catalyst to accelerate your spiritual growth and rekindle your love for Christ.

But does such a thing exist?

Yes. And remarkably it's something we likely know about and participate in regularly, but the meaning has been lost. What we're talking about is the Lord's Table, Communion. Luke describes it simply as "the breaking of bread" in Acts 2:42. Paul refers to it variously in his letters as "communion," "the table of the Lord," "the Lord's supper," and the "eucharist" in 1 Corinthians 10–11. It is based on the time that Jesus spent in the Upper Room supping with His disciples on the eve of His arrest, but for the attentive Christian, it's not just the commemoration of that historical meal. Communion is the best safeguard against doctrinal error, the best defense against apathy and lethargy, the best motivation for love and excitement for the Redeemer, and the best window into the depth and accessibility of gospel truth.

If that sounds to you like slick marketing hype, you don't understand the power of Communion.

We've talked about worshipping Jesus in the fellowship of His church. It's an awesome experience, but within that context Communion was intended to be a point at which every Christian comes regularly to recalibrate, refocus, reenergize, renew, and recommit. The experience at the table—when we remember Jesus and examine our lives in light of His sacrifice on our behalf—was also meant to expand and give fullness to our experience of Christ throughout the week. Communion is the perfect place to uneclipse the Son in your life, expelling the distractions, eradicating obstacles that cloak His glory.

As effective as it is, it's no wonder Communion is embattled. A hundred years ago J. C. Ryle said, "It's impossible to overstate the importance of the Lord's Supper. I owe to a strong and growing conviction that error about the Lord's Supper is one of the most common and most dangerous errors of the present day. Perhaps no part of the Christian religion is so thoroughly misunderstood than the Lord's Supper; and on no other point have there been so many disputes, strife, for over 2,000 years in the church's history."[1] Debates about who can participate in it, who can administer it, and what it really means and accomplishes fill the pages of church history with a litany of movements and perspectives. But in God's design, the simple and profound lesson is hard to miss. There at the Table of the Lord, all the basic elements for growing your faith await.

THE FIGHT AGAINST FORGETTING

The last meal Jesus had with His disciples was unlike any they had shared before.

Something was up.

Matthew records the scene succinctly in Matthew 26:

> While they were eating, Jesus took some bread, and after a bless-
> ing, He broke it and gave it to the disciples, and said, "Take,
> eat; this is My body." And when He had taken a cup and given
> thanks, He gave it to them, saying, "Drink from it, all of you; for
> this is My blood of the covenant, which is poured out for many
> for forgiveness of sins. But I say to you, I will not drink of this
> fruit of the vine from now on until that day when I drink it new
> with you in My Father's kingdom" (vv. 26–29).

These were remarkable words from the Lord, which no doubt
charged the room with dread and wonder and not a little confusion.

John was also there, and his account explains that this was the time
when Judas was identified as the Lord's betrayer. Judas got up during the
meal and left to go do his evil deed (John 13:2, 21–30). Interestingly,
while Paul was not in attendance that night, he gives us perhaps the
fullest application and explanation of its significance. In 1 Corinthians
11:23–26 he writes:

> For I received from the Lord that which I also delivered to you,
> that the Lord Jesus in the night in which He was betrayed took
> bread; and when He had given thanks, He broke it and said,
> "This is My body, which is for you; do this in remembrance of
> Me." In the same way *He took* the cup also after supper, saying,
> "This cup is the new covenant in My blood; do this, as often as
> you drink *it*, in remembrance of Me." For as often as you eat this
> bread and drink the cup, you proclaim the Lord's death until He
> comes.

Twice in these verses Paul refers to Jesus as the Lord. The *Lord* did
this; He established that which He wanted the disciples to perpetuate as

a "remembrance" that would continue to "proclaim the Lord's death" to the end of the age.

The Passover celebration is flooded with the power of memory. Paul links the commemorative nature of that miracle in Egypt (Exodus 12; Deuteronomy 16) with the recollection of the death of Christ. In that upper room Jesus took the Passover bread, broke it, and passed a piece to each of His disciples. Whereas the Passover bread represented physical deliverance, this bread would take on a greater symbolism: greater in truth, greater in meaning. God was about to deliver them from their sins just as He delivered His people from Egypt and from the hands of Pharaoh. Jesus was prescribing His very body and blood sacrificed on a cruel Roman cross for the sins of those who would believe.

Before we move on, consider for a moment the lengths to which God instructed the Israelites to go in order that they might never forget their deliverance from Egypt on the night of the Passover. Exodus 12 describes the whole affair. The week before Passover every family was to go out and pick their Passover lamb. A sweet, young, unblemished lamb. They were to bring it into their house for five days. It's fair to say that during that time the family would develop an attachment to the cuddly creature. *How perfect it is! How innocent!* But at the end of those five days, the father would bring the family together. He would get down on his knee to cup the lamb's chin in his hand. With the other hand he would take a long, razor-sharp blade, look up at the glistening eyes of his wife and children, and say something like, "We deserve death, the angel of death, but in grace and mercy the Lord has passed over us. In our place He pours out His wrath on this lamb."

With that he would slice the lamb's neck, severing the veins and arteries. With blood spewing everywhere, the dying sounds of aspiration would fill the room. As the heart would lose pressure and slow, the animal would begin to go into spasms and gasp for breath. Its legs would instinctively move as if to run away from the trauma. Falling onto its side it would go into a final death quiver. It was horrific.

And they did this every year...to remember. Fast-forward to New

Testament time in the wilderness of Judea. Jesus was coming to be baptized by His cousin, John the Baptist. John points to Jesus coming toward him and announces to the watching crowd, "Behold, the Lamb of God who takes away the sin of the world!" (John 1:29). A profound connection was being made. The Passover Lamb would be the Son of God slain for sinners. And make no mistake, that cross was far more graphic and far more horrific than any Passover sacrifice. How much more critical is it for us to remember this sacrifice.

One of the first criticisms and waves of persecution of Christianity was based on a misunderstanding of the nature of Communion. First-century Romans accused believers of a form of cannibalism when they heard that they partook of the body and blood of Jesus. After all, Jesus did say, *this is my body and blood,* and Paul said to repeat the supper as often as the church met. But did the disciples really believe they were experiencing cannibalism during this last supper? No. He was obviously speaking metaphorically; they understood that, and so did Paul. This is plain from the little phrase in 1 Corinthians 11:24: "Do this in remembrance of Me." He is not recrucified. He is remembered. The Lord's Table is to be a memorial, a vivid and powerful reminder.

This brings us to the crux of the whole matter: Jesus knew that His followers would forget Him. The apostles who lived with Him and walked with Him were likely to simply move on in the business of life. Remember that after the resurrection we find some of them back at their fishing trade. Are we any better than them? How long can we live, how many seconds and minutes and hours and days can we go, without reflecting back and remembering the death that brought us spiritual life? In the press of life, we're in a fight against forgetfulness. The most devastating and damaging thing to forget is the meaning of it all, and that's Jesus Himself and the death with which He served God and man. How often do you stop and think about the death of Jesus for your sin? How long can you go without meditating on the cross? God understands we forget. That's why He put Communion in our path.

If we are obedient, we will not fail to come to the table. And each time we do we should see the gospel in rich and tangible symbolism. Paul writes in verse 25, "He took the cup also after supper, saying, 'This cup is the new covenant in My blood.'" This is a picture of the death, burial, and resurrection of the Son of God. Drink it and remember. Jesus drank the cup of the wrath of God so we could drink the cup of satisfaction, calling to mind the Lamb that could not be spared.

We must understand that Communion is a high vantage from which to get a better view of the glory of the cross. It should humble us, cheer us, encourage us, sanctify us, and restrain us from sin. Beyond that, Paul says in verse 26, "For as often as you eat this bread and drink the cup, you proclaim the Lord's death until He comes." We partakers are proclaimers, preaching the gospel to each other and a watching world until He returns to unveil completely His precious bride.

THE EXAMINATION TABLE

Sometimes remembering Jesus is painful. Paul makes this very point in 1 Corinthians 11:27–28: "Therefore whoever eats the bread or drinks the cup of the Lord in an unworthy manner, shall be guilty of the body and the blood of the Lord. But a man must examine himself, and in so doing he is to eat of the bread and drink of the cup." When you come face-to-face with the Lord at the cross, at the table, you must become keenly aware of the sin for which Jesus died. And the only way to do that is to first examine yourself. Again, J. C. Ryle says, "A sense of our own unworthiness is the best worthiness we can bring to the Lord's table. A deep feeling of our own entire indebtedness to Christ for all we have and hope for and is the best feeling we can bring with us."[2]

When the Son is eclipsed by the sin in your life, the table seems like drudgery. But if you partake of it in such a state, it may just prove lethal. Ryle adds that it should be forever remembered "that the man who is unfit for the Lord's Supper is unfit to die."[3] Why? Verses 29–30 say, "For he who eats and drinks, eats and drinks judgment to himself if he does not judge the body rightly. For this reason many among you are weak and sick, and a number sleep." To celebrate the Lord's Table without an examined life is to mock the cross, and God will judge. We may be afflicted with weakness or sickness, which always brings us back to Him. Or He could decide that if we're going to continue to take Communion in an unworthy manner, He's just going to bring us home to heaven.

You may say, "Is it really that serious?"

Yes, if you celebrate the Lord's death while simultaneously clinging to sin. This equates to mocking His death for your sin. Verse 32 continues, "But when we are judged, we are disciplined by the Lord so that we will not be condemned along with the world." God's firm hand of discipline prevents us from facing His wrath along with unredeemed mankind. After all, God already poured His wrath out on Christ for us as a substitute. That's about as serious as anything can get. Communion is an opportunity to pore over the conduct of your life and, to the best of your abilities by the light of Scripture and conscience, to examine the thoughts of your heart with an eye to being holy.

Is there a sin that is unconfessed? Is there sin that's not repented of? Is there sin that has gone unchecked? Are there habits in your life that are sinful, in which you are seeing no progress? Here is the place to renounce them, renounce Satan and his associates in your heart, and cling to Jesus and His sacrifice on your behalf. At the table you can enjoy the feast of God's mercy, the tastes of His forgiveness, the flavor of His love.

AN EVENT AND A COMPASS

Many throughout history have died for the sanctity of the Lord's Table, the opportunity to remember Jesus.

For sixty-two months, Mary Tudor reigned in England. We know her today as "Bloody Mary." For forty-six horrific months, from February 4, 1555 to November 10, 1558, this Catholic queen killed Protestants by the hundreds. What made her so angry with them? They believed Communion was about remembering Jesus and examining one's life rather than what she held: that Communion reduplicated the crucifixion of Christ during the Mass. Even when given opportunity to recant and believe the Roman Catholic view of Communion, many of the Protestants wouldn't. Two-hundred and twenty-seven men and fifty-six women were burned alive over the preciousness of the Lord's Table. For them, a proper understanding of the gospel led to a proper understanding of Communion; a proper understanding of Communion led to execution.[4]

The first preacher to die for his understanding of the Lord's Table was John Rogers. He burned in Smithfield on February 4, a very cold Monday in 1555. They led him from prison to the field across the street from his church, set up the stake, put bundles of wood around him, and set this martyr ablaze. It's said that the night before his execution he slept so soundly that the jailer had to startle him in the morning to even wake him up. Asked one final time to deny his understanding of Communion or be put to death, he refused. As he was marched to Smithfield to the stake, he paused to speak with his wife and children standing in the crowd. She had been refused permission to see him in prison, but she was given this final meeting with him at the stake. Nursing John's tenth child, Adrianna Rogers stood with their children encouraging him to remain faithful as he perished in the flames.[5]

John Hooper, also a Protestant preacher, burned in a similar manner. Seven thousand people came to watch, to see if he would recant the gospel and be spared. He would not.[6]

On Friday, March 30, 1555, Robert Ferrar too was burned at the stake. He told a friend the day before his execution that if he saw Ferrar stir and flinch from pain while his body was burned, he could reject everything Ferrar had taught about the gospel. The time came when he burned. Ferrar never flinched and sang songs of praise to the bitter end.[7]

John Philpot came to Smithfield to be burned on December 18, 1555. At the stake he knelt down and said, "I will pay my vows in thee, O Smithfield." He then kissed the stake and said, "Shall I disdain to suffer at this stake seeing that my Redeemer did not refuse to suffer a most vile death on the Cross for me?"[8]

Thomas Cranmer was told to recant his view of Communion or be burned alive. Unlike these other men, this Protestant recanted. Queen Mary had promised Cranmer a full pardon if he recanted but went back on her word, informing him that he would still be burned. After a few days under the sentence of execution, he sent word that he was going to recant his recantation.

The execution time came and he was bound to the stake. As the flames climbed his body, he put his right hand down into the fire. He wanted the hand that signed the recantation of the truth of the gospel to be destroyed first. It was burned to a stump as his body gave up its soul.[9]

Perotine Cowchen wasn't a preacher. She was just a lady in the community. A disagreement arose between her and a loyal Catholic woman. The woman turned Perotine in to the authorities as one disloyal to the Queen's doctrine of the Mass. At eight months pregnant, she was tied together with her mother and her sister at the stake to be burned. Jasper Ridley records what happened: "When the fire was lit, the heat of the fire caused Perotine to give birth to the baby, a son, who fell on the fagots [wood bundles] while the flames burned around him. One of the spectators rushed forward to save the baby and pulled him out of the fire and laid him on the grass; a man in arms picked the baby up; he was handed from one official to the other till he was given to the Sheriff in charge of the execution. The Sheriff ordered his men to throw the baby back into the fire and he was burned with his mother, his grandmother, and his aunt."[10]

Why do I recount these atrocities? So we see the importance of the Lord's Table not only as an event, but as a compass to orient our hearts. These people could have avoided death if they would have simply shrugged off the importance of Communion. We think lightly of Communion when our hearts have lost track of the true north of Christ and His cross.

How do you uneclipse Jesus? You hold precious His death and remember His greatness.

How do you hold that He is precious? By examining your life and seeing your sinfulness and loving His sacrifice on the cross on your behalf.

Where does that come into focus most clearly?

During the Lord's Supper.

How does Communion function in your life? It functions as a catalyst, as a checkpoint, but also as a pattern of living. Remember Jesus; examine yourself; repeat. As you do this, you'll find fresh reminders that He's alive and He's going to come back.

THE PROMISE OF HIS COMING

A lot of crackers and juice have been served in the two thousand years since Christ instituted Communion.

But it won't continue forever. As Paul explained carefully, we "proclaim the Lord's death until He comes" (1 Corinthians 11:26). If I told you that today Jesus is going to return in the clouds and call His saints to Himself, would that thought bring you joy? Or does it make you shudder with fear and think of all of the things you've got to get right with the Lord before He comes?

The elements of the Lord's Supper, not just the bread and the cup, but the elements of remembering Jesus and examining yourself, are to function as that reminder. Jesus is coming. We don't want to be like the people in 2 Peter 3:3–10 who say in essence, *Where is the promise of His coming?* Who say, *Come on, we've heard He's coming for a long time and He's not here yet.* Peter answers them, *Beware, the Lord doesn't count time like we count time. A day, a thousand years, it's all the same to Him; He's outside of time.*

The Father does have the date circled on His calendar when He is going to tell Christ, "Go get Your bride, the people that You purchased with Your blood." And when He returns will He find us ready? Think about it for a moment. The primary commands associated with the Lord's Table are simply to examine yourself and remember Jesus. Communion then is really a microcosm of what all of Christian living should be. Think of how different your perspective would be if your thinking were dominated by self-examination that led to repentance and remembering Jesus that led to worship. An examined, worshipful life says always, "Come, Lord Jesus! Be completely uneclipsed to me forever!"

COME TO THE TABLE

My wife is an amazing cook. One of our favorite meals occurs almost every Saturday morning. She makes pancakes and bacon. The smell of that breakfast permeates the house, and our sons and I can't wait to hear her say, "Come to the table!"

We love that meal. Some of our best family times happen around that table on Saturday mornings. We are unhurried, undistracted, and hungry.

When the glorified church meets for the Lord's Supper in heaven, it is He Himself who will say, "Come to the table!" But Communion is not a meal for the body; it is a feast for the soul. At this table we sit as unworthy guests by the invitation of Jesus' merit. If we will approach that time unhurried in our worship, undistracted in our attention, and hungry for righteousness, it will amplify spiritual growth and insight like nothing else. Communion is like a divine X-ray that exposes what's really inside. It realigns everything. The table emanates the aroma of heaven and makes our mouths water for its delights. It allows us the moments we need to turn our eyes upon Jesus, to look full in His wonderful face. Then the things of earth will indeed grow strangely dim in the light of His glory and grace.

SOMETHING YOU CAN'T STOP TALKING ABOUT

There's a sense in which you can hear an eclipse.

Cycle back for a moment to the story with which I began this book, watching a solar eclipse with my first-grade class. We were twenty kids that *never* stopped talking, much to our teacher's chagrin, but when the light of the sun became dim, our voices were stilled. We collectively held our breath. In a shared silence we watched in wonder as everything we thought we knew about nature was challenged.

After a few seconds of silence, we broke into shouting. We all pointed up at the sky, and turned to our friends exclaiming, "Did you see that?" The rest of the day Mrs. Cunningham tried to teach math and spelling in vain. Classroom decorum, like the sun itself, had disappeared as we overflowed with endless exuberance about what we had seen in the sky that morning.

When I got home, I couldn't wait to see my dad to tell him about it. After all, he was the one who had turned my interest toward the sky. The eclipse had so captured my heart that I couldn't stop thinking about it, which meant I couldn't stop talking about it.

Jesus said, "His mouth speaks from that which fills his heart" (Luke 6:45). It is axiomatic that what we love, we talk about. Finding out what you love is easy enough; simply listen to yourself talk. Our emotions capture thoughts, ideas, and concepts, and store them in our hearts. As we meditate on them, they bubble over into our speech.

What fills your heart, even at this moment?

Those around you know already. Your parents, your friends, your wife, your children, and those in your church probably have a very realistic understanding of what you love. They know if your heart is flooded with the light of Christ or drowning in the cares and pursuits of the world. The recurring themes that fill our conversations do not lie.

The danger of worldliness is seen in its power to eclipse our love for Jesus, and perhaps nowhere is this more apparent than in our speech. If your heart is captured by sports, clothes, games, cars, or self, then Jesus is crowded out of your speech.

But as Jesus rises to the surface of your affections, He will become uneclipsed in your life. When this happens, He will become the One you can't stop talking about. Your heart will overflow with the truth of who He is and what He has done.

This is the essence of evangelism. When Jesus fills your heart, you can't help but tell others about Him.

"ME, A PRIEST?"

You probably don't walk around thinking of yourself as a priest. You don't wear a silly collar and you have not taken a vow of celibacy. You recognize that you are not the arbiter of all things godly. In Jewish terms, you've never prepared an animal for sacrifice upon an altar. You haven't gone to seminary, and you are most likely not a Levite by birth.

This is why Peter's announcement that every believer is a priest is so strange to us. He writes, "But you are a chosen race, a royal priesthood, a holy nation, a people for God's own possession" (1 Peter 2:9). Understanding election and sanctification helps us understand how he can call believers "a chosen race" and "a holy nation." But how can Peter call those who have no priestly training and perform no sacerdotal duties "a royal priesthood"?

The answer lies in the truth that God only has one people. God never set forth one way of salvation in the Old Testament for Jews and a separate way of salvation in the New Testament for Christians. And while Levites were priests by birth, their lineage did not give them special access to God's saving grace. Rather, for all time, anyone who comes to God must come to Him through faith and via the appropriate sacrifice.

When there is sin, there is punishment, and this punishment can only be met by the shedding of blood. In the garden, an animal's blood was spilt to atone for the first sin. After the flood, Noah sacrificed animals to atone for the sin of the world. And priests found their calling in the seemingly perpetual slaughter of animals for the sins of the nation of Israel.

Though a priest was a butcher by occupation, he had another, greater function. Every sacrifice that a priest performed served as an indicator to the people of Israel. On the one hand, it pointed up to the God who designed the world such that sin could be forgiven through the shedding of blood. On the other hand, each sacrifice also pointed forward to the Messiah, the ultimate sacrifice, who would put an end to the sacrificial system.

The death of Jesus not only made the old covenant obsolete (Hebrews 8:13), but it ended the inherited office of the priest. From that moment on, nobody could become a priest by birth. The role of pointing people to the God who forgives sin and to the sacrifice that provides atonement fell to this new class of people. This group would be a royal priesthood, made up of all believers in the death and resurrection of Jesus.

No longer would the priesthood be all male, and all from the line of Levi. No longer would God give His people a priest to make intercession, because He gave us Jesus, the Intercessor (Romans 8:34). No longer does the reminder of sacrifice come from a specific tribe of Jews, but now it comes from everyone who has faith that Jesus is the Messiah.

Believers are a part of Christ's royal priesthood. We don't perform sacrifices; we tell of the great sacrifice of Jesus. We do this not because it's in our job description, but because it is the overflow of our hearts. We cannot contain it.

REDEFINING EVANGELISM

What is evangelism?

Many Christians conceive of evangelism as the process of presenting a series of laws or a scripted program. Evangelism is often morphed into a memorized formula to be conveyed, accepted, and repeated, as if the gospel could be contained in a series of bullet points or captured on a billboard.

But an abridged and alliterated gospel presentation is noticeably absent from the pages of the New Testament. Instead of conveying the message of salvation through a plan, God has given the world a people––a priesthood—for the purpose of evangelism. Peter describes evangelism as simply proclaiming "the excellencies of Him who has called you out of darkness into His marvelous light" (1 Peter 2:9).

Jesus not only saved us, but He made us into a priesthood for the purpose of proclamation. He saved us so that we can tell the world of His excellencies. We who were once blinded by sin have come squinting and stumbling out of darkness into the glorious dawn of Christ. Now we are proclaimers to the world: There is a light more marvelous than the darkness of sin! It is a holy light heralded by holy people, a royal priesthood.

The glory of this truth is often obscured behind evangelism training programs. While some programs are genuinely helpful, it is important to remember that the gospel is not a plan but a Person. Witnessing is sharing what we've seen of Jesus, simply proclaiming the facets of His ineffable person.

DO GOOD, FEEL GOOD

Between 2002 and 2005 The National Study of Youth and Religion conducted extensive research on the religious lives of American young people. The conclusions of the project were alarming regarding the students graduating from evangelical youth ministries. Books and articles were generated to interpret and respond to the data.

One researcher concludes: "American young people are theoretically fine with religious faith. But it does not concern them very much. And it's not durable enough to survive long after they graduate from high school."[1] The study "reveals a theological fault line running underneath American churches: an adherence to a 'do good, feel good' spirituality, that has little to do with the triune God and the Christian tradition, and even less with loving Jesus enough to follow Him into the world."[2]

If these conclusions are accurate, there are serious ramifications for the future of Christ's church. Youth groups are producing a nondoctrinal Christianity, a feel-good and do-good spirituality. Unthinkably, for many the Christian faith has been reduced to a gospel of niceness.[3]

The question is, where did this spurious version of Christianity come from? How was it seeded to an entire generation? Certainly there are many causes, but one that stands out to me is the prevalence of pragmatic witnessing. Much youth evangelism over the preceding decades has focused on confronting outward behavior, such as drugs, sex, and alcohol. The result is that witnessing has eroded into a call to "shape up," rather than a demand to worship Jesus.

Peter said that Christians are called to proclaim the excellencies of Jesus. Evangelism is simply proclaiming the things that are noteworthy and excellent about Jesus. If you know enough to be saved, you know enough to evangelize. Just keep talking about Jesus from the overflow of your heart, and the gospel will be declared.

This is not meant to minimize the importance of explaining the necessary elements of the gospel, such as the imputation of sins, or the crucifixion and resurrection of Jesus. But if you simply tell others about what Jesus has done for you, these elements will be presented.

Can you talk very long about Jesus without going to the cross? Can you talk very long about Jesus without talking about His sinlessness? Can you talk very long about Jesus without saying He was a man whom God raised from the dead? Can you talk very much about Jesus without saying He was and is God? For Peter, the excellencies of Christ are the substance of the gospel message, and this kind of evangelism is more comprehensive than you think.

Paul also evangelized in this way. For example, in 1 Corinthians 15:3–4, Paul sums up the facts of the gospel: "Christ died for our sins according to the Scriptures, and that He was buried, and that He was raised on the third day according to the Scriptures." In the next two verses he describes how this was verified by witnesses. Paul's gospel was simple and straightforward: the Messiah died for sins according to the Scriptures. Don't miss the fact that the central focus of Paul's preaching was Jesus: who He was (the Messiah), what He did (He died for sin), how it was verified (He was raised from the dead).

When evangelism comes from the overflow of our hearts, as it did for the persecutor-turned-preacher Paul, we long to take others on a tour of the excellencies and virtues of Jesus. We explain who He is, what His attributes mean in our lives, and how He has proved Himself sufficient in our every need. He relates to us, yet He doesn't naturally act like you and I would act. He changed our lives, He is now praying for us, and He gives us hope in the face of adversity and confidence in the face of death. He offers peace, assurance, confidence, hope, security, solidarity, fellowship, forgiveness, redemption, fullfillment, and purpose.

It's important as we gush about Jesus, though, that we don't present the benefits of being a Christian as being better than Jesus Himself. Imagine if I extolled all the benefits of married life without ever mentioning the love I have for my wife. Evangelism that explains what "belief" offers—rather than who Jesus is—falls into this trap. Tell others about the Person they will know, rather than what they will get. After all, as we've already explored, we are the bride of Christ. Do we gather together to worship the benefits package or the Great and Coming King who has redeemed us to God? When we get to know what's great about Jesus, we talk about Him.

With that being said, it's also critical for us to prayerfully rely on the Spirit in our evangelism. This work isn't always easy. In Colossians 4:2–4, the apostle Paul writes, "Devote yourselves to prayer, keeping alert in it with an attitude of thanksgiving; praying at the same time for us as well, that God will open up to us a door for the word, so that we may speak forth the mystery of Christ, for which I have also been imprisoned; that I may make it clear in the way I ought to speak."

Here is Paul, gifted and emboldened as few others in all the record of Scripture, submitting his prayer request. In the context, this "word" is a synonym for the gospel. He says in essence, *Pray He'll open to us a door to articulate and present the gospel.* Then in verses 5–6 he writes, "Conduct yourselves with wisdom toward outsiders, making the most of the opportunity. Let your speech always be with grace, as though seasoned with salt, so that you will know how you should respond to each person." The apostle Paul serves as our example here, requesting prayer and encouraging us to have our tongues loaded with the grace of God for any opportunity. That should encourage us all. If even Paul is asking for prayer for gospel opportunities, we understand our own fears and our own dependence.

AN UNMISTAKABLE ACCENT

When you trace the presentations of the gospel throughout Scripture, you discover that they all have the same accent: Jesus. The Bible knows nothing of a gospel that offers salvation through good deeds. The true gospel stresses Jesus, not noble feelings. This is because the Bible was written by those whose hearts overflowed with love for the excellencies of Jesus.

We can go back as far as the day of Pentecost to the first Christian sermon ever preached. Peter begins:

"Men of Israel, listen to these words: Jesus the Nazarene, a man attested to you by God with miracles and wonders and signs which God performed through Him in your midst, just as you yourselves know—this Man, delivered over by the predetermined plan and foreknowledge of God, you nailed to a cross by the hands of godless men and put Him to death. But God raised Him up again, putting an end to the agony of death, since it was impossible for Him to be held in its power." (Acts 2:22–24)

On the southern steps of the temple mount in Jerusalem, the first sermon ever preached was filled with Christology—His sovereign power, His miraculous abilities, His substitutionary death, and His resurrection glory. Absent are tips on how to improve your life or how to be more successful. Instead, the gathered masses heard a message that was truly good news because it was centered on the only good person: Jesus.

The accent of Peter's preaching was hardly unique. The rest of Acts shows that Jesus was the focus of every evangelistic opportunity. In one of the New Testament's most well-known evangelistic encounters, an Ethiopian was reading messianic prophecy and was convicted (Acts 8:26–39). When Philip approached his chariot, the Ethiopian had one simple request: "Please tell me, of whom does the prophet say this?" Philip then "opened his mouth, and beginning from this Scripture he preached Jesus" to the pilgrim.

In the next chapter, Acts records the conversion of Saul, who would become Paul, the church's most fruitful evangelist. God converted Saul by giving him a vision of the risen Messiah that was so glorious that Saul was blinded for three days. But when his sight was finally restored, "immediately he began to proclaim Jesus in the synagogues, saying, 'He is the Son of God'" (Acts 9:20). Paul's accent gave him away. He had seen Jesus, the Son of God.

The apostle Peter likewise had Jesus-centered evangelism. When he preached to the Gentiles, the theme of his gospel presentation was "peace through Jesus Christ (He is Lord of all)" (Acts 10:36).

Jesus was the focus of all New Testament evangelism. There were no plans, no steps, and no tests. Never once does the Bible present evangelism as exhorting believers to do better or to feel better about themselves. Rather, the chorus resounds, "Jesus, Jesus, Jesus."

But where does that leave you? Do you know enough about Jesus to tell people what is excellent about Him? Do you spend time in secret, secluded moments thinking about the sweeping excellence of His nature? Do you spend time getting a better view of Jesus, or are there too many things eclipsing Him? Are you ready to speak of Christ and for Christ in any company and whenever you have opportunity? Are you watching for a chance in every conversation for something that you can use to turn the conversation back to Jesus, diverting the conversation from vanity and the mundane, to the ultimate reality of the living Savior?

THE GOSPEL IS JESUS

It should be obvious by now that the gospel is Jesus. The word means "good news." This good news is that the Messiah promised in the Old Testament is the Lord. We have a Savior, Jesus, who is at the center of our affections. Remember what we talked about back in chapter 3, that Jesus Himself defined eternal life as knowing Him in John 17:3. When we truly know Him, we can usher others out of the eclipse of sin and into the hope of the gospel. When we know Him, we can and will proclaim Him.

John Owen captures this in a poignant sentence that compels me in my own worship: "He is no Christian who lives not much in the meditation of the mediation of Christ, and especially of the acts of it."[4] If you live in wonder of the cross and meditate on Jesus as the mediator between God and people, you will be a person whose heart overflows to others with your affection for Him.

THE INTRODUCTION

On a cold morning in February of 2010, Richard Code left a note on his landlady's door: "If I'm not back by Monday, please call the authorities." Along with the note were a set of GPS coordinates and a list of the supplies he had with him.

Don't let that professional touch fool you, however. Code was no expert.

In the weeks and months leading up to this midwinter bivouac in the Muskoka wilderness of Canada, Code had begun to follow a new cable television show called *Survivorman*. The premise of the show is simple. The host heads out into the wilderness to demonstrate that being knowledgeable and prepared can actually save your life.

Code was a big fan. As he set out that morning, he felt certain he could brave the elements, applying what he'd learned from the show. Four days later, his body was recovered by helicopter in an area that was no longer accessible by foot, thanks to a blanket of heavy snowfall. His solar blanket did not prove adequate, and, unable to start a fire with the wet timber, he succumbed to hypothermia.[1]

Richard Code was an enthusiast with little experience and almost no training. He set out to emulate a professional who had all the advantages of years of instruction and practice, and he found himself overcome by the cruel realities of climate.

It's a tragic story, but it highlights the basic principle that knowing *about* something doesn't mean you know how to do it. Seeing it done is a world away from doing it. Enthusiasm only gets you so far.

Think about this principle in the context of our book. It works on every level.

A thin emulation of Christianness is not the same as worshipping Jesus.

Attending church, going to Bible studies, downloading sermons, listening to Christian music, having believing friends—these things don't necessarily equip you to worship Jesus.

A zeal for the ideas and principles and culture of Christianity does not equate to worshipping your Savior in spirit and in truth.

Appreciating a well-crafted sermon, digging into a book, even being able to explain a theological truth or memorize a passage of Scripture does not ensure that you're living it.

Even knowing that Jesus is eclipsed in your life does not mean you understand how to, or are even willing to, remove that eclipse. You may still be moving behind the shadows, going through the motions.

Life is too short and eternity is too long to end up the spiritual equivalent of Richard Code. It's time for us to move to application. The titles of the first and last chapters of this book are not a mistake. We began with the conclusion—that the all-too-easily-eclipsed Jesus is the centrality of our faith. And now we will finish with the introduction—the way to set out uneclipsing the Son in your life.

THE WORLD WAS NOT WORTHY

In the twelfth chapter of Hebrews, the author lays down a succinct and stunningly simple way of putting into action all that we have learned in this book. To get into it, you need to understand the broader context of Hebrews, so let me give you the warp-speed tour of the first eleven chapters. The original hearers were very much like those of us trying to uneclipse Jesus. They were well versed in Scripture; they understood the law and the prophets; they understood the gospel—but they had fallen into a deep, deep spiritual lethargy. They were lazy.

They came to believe that because they understood some gospel truth, that was enough. While there were some unbelievers in the mix, the primary target of his letter was a group of believers who were slipping, losing traction in their walk with Christ. The message to the Hebrews reduces down to two main ideas: The person and the work of Christ, and staying faithful to Him. Even if you can articulate the nuances of the gospel, it's still imperative to remain faithful to those truths, to live them out, to not be lulled into lethargy because you think, *I understand, therefore I've arrived.* Understanding and appreciating spiritual truth is pretty easy; moving the principles into your life is an entirely different exercise.

By the time we come to Hebrews 11, the message has reached a critical and urgent crescendo. Chapter 11 turns to the subject of faith and describes a list of people who have lived it out faithfully going back to the earliest days of God's dealings with mankind. These are men and women who believed what God had said, taking Him at His Word, even when their circumstances would seem to dictate that it was time to cut and run or cower in fear. Even before Christ had entered the world, these were people who saw beyond the shadowland and lived in the substance of things they hadn't even seen and couldn't imagine.

Everyone asks deep in their hearts, *Can anyone actually live out this life of faith?* Hebrews 11 answers that question with an emphatic, "Yes! You're not alone. This is doable." These people lived life with the invisible God by simply believing Him and taking Him at His Word, just as we looked at earlier in chapter 6. And it made the difference in their lives. The path for living by faith has been paved before us, worn smooth by the feet of people like you and me who aligned their lives with the promises of God.

Hebrews 12 picks up the trail and moves it into our time, where we have the amazing honor to look back at the cross and resurrection of Jesus. The author says it's time to commit, take up the banner of faith, and go forward. Be inspired by your forebears and move out: "Therefore, since we have so great a cloud of witnesses surrounding us, let us also lay aside every encumbrance and the sin which so easily entangles us, and let us run with endurance the race that is set before us, fixing our eyes on Jesus, the author and perfecter of faith, who for the joy set before Him endured the cross, despising the shame, and has sat down at the right hand of the throne of God. For consider Him who has endured such hostility by sinners against Himself, so that you will not grow weary and lose heart" (vv. 1–3).

If you want to see Jesus have first place in your life, first place in your focus, first place in your affections, you have to be inspired. The passage describes an audience watching a race. In the grandstands we find a "great...cloud of witnesses," a dense mass of those who have been there and done that standing together, testifying to the feats of life that can be accomplished when an individual lives by faith. The record of their lives is a record of responding to God's commands in the affirmative and acting on them, come what may. Among them were Abel, Enoch, Noah, Abraham, Sarah, Jacob, Moses, David, Samuel—all "men of whom the world was not worthy" (11:38).

EVERYTHING MUST GO

It's appropriate at this juncture to consider what the record of *your* life will be. Can the world claim you as its own, or will you find your voice in this chorus of the faithful? Since these people are "surrounding us," and they are the success stories that we want to follow, like them we'll need to "lay aside every encumbrance and the sin which so easily entangles us."

Everything must go. The imagery here is pretty graphic. Literally the sense is *Let us strip down so that no clothes hinder our run*. The author is again drawing on the imagery of stripping down for a race. Have you ever watched a track meet or an Olympic race? If so, you may have noticed that the uniforms for running have become increasingly smaller and tighter. The goal is simple: wear as little as possible so that nothing has the possibility of reducing your effectiveness as you race. Keep in mind, they didn't have Lycra back then; they raced completely naked. Everything was put off.

What a perfect illustration! You will never see a runner kneeling on the starting blocks wearing a fireman's suit with a giant helmet and oxygen tank on his back. Likewise, we must lay everything aside if we hope to compete in the race of faith. The encumbrances he's described are sins and sinful distractions—specific, individual, personal, recognized sins. And we might add that any and all distractions ultimately *are* sins if they're keeping us from the worship of Jesus. These types of things cannot fail to trip us up and weigh us down. Anything that is hurtful to your soul must be laid aside if you would see and live in the glory of Christ as He intends.

I can never read these verses without thinking of the time my "friends" in freshman physical science tied my shoelaces to my desk while I was working. The bell rang, I jumped up—and instantly kissed the floor. That's the sense we get in these verses. You're going nowhere fast. You're tied up, entangled. You can't move forward until you take care of what's holding you back. The question is, do you have the spiritual awareness to understand what it is that's bogging you down? Can you step back and say, "The pursuit of this, the enjoyment of that, my relationship with this person—is hurtful, rather than helpful, in my pursuit of Christ"?

These encumbrances are not the same for everybody, as we examined in chapter 7. First John 2:16 describes three broad categories of sin: the lust of the flesh, the lust of the eyes, and the boastful pride of life. But there are specific sins that entangle you which may not entangle another person. For some it's lust; for others it's gluttony; for others it's lying, exaggerating, anger, jealousy, covetousness, or envy. For some it's laziness; for others it's a love of liberties, drunkenness, or gossip.

Can you identify what entangles you, what's heavy around your feet and holding you back? J. C. Ryle said that "The gates of Heaven are broad enough to receive the worst of sinners, but too narrow to admit the smallest grain of unforsaken sin."[2] He'll take any sinner, but you have to be willing to leave your sin.

Jesus didn't hold back from calling us to the most radical kind of "laying aside" of sins. Matthew 5:29–30 says, "If your right eye makes you stumble, tear it out and throw it from you.... If your right hand makes you stumble, cut it off and throw it from you...." It would have been enough to pluck out your eye; you can't see once your eye is on the ground. But Jesus won't have us stop there; it must be fetched and thrown away. Christ knew that the stakes for our souls are high. No measure is too unthinkable. Anything and everything that gets in the way of pursuing His glory must go.

J. C. Ryle, commenting on this passage, declared, "Oh, what a condemnation there is here for all those easy-going persons, who seem to think they may pass their time as they please, and yet be numbered with the saints in glory. Are those who show less earnestness about their souls than about their earthly amusements, and those who have much to tell you about this world's business but nothing about heaven, and those who think nothing of neglecting the commonest helps toward Zion and count it much to give religion a few Sunday thoughts, are these men running the Christian race and straining every nerve after the prize?"[3]

Is your faith merely a few thoughts about Jesus on Sunday? Are you straining after the prize? Consider that it's only when you start running, trying to live a holy life and see past the eclipse, that you even recognize that you have encumbrances. I didn't know my feet were tied to that chair until I got up and started to walk. You have to get started, you have to give it some effort, you have to focus on Christ, and then see what's revealed. Only those who are pursuing Jesus are truly sensitive to what's holding them back. You have to start running!

GO TIME

Hebrews 12:1 contains the powerful command that drives this entire passage: "Let us run with endurance the race that is set before us." The throngs have gathered in the amphitheater, watching this race. You've put off your known sins and other distractions. It's go time. Will you run?

Don't overcomplicate the metaphor. You're not in some kind of competition with other Christians. The race here is won by simply finishing, taking your place with the other witnesses "of whom the world was not worthy." But to be assured of the finish, you must "run with endurance." This is a marathon, not a sprint. Run with patient, enduring effort those final strides to glory. Notice that last phrase of verse one defines the course: it's the one "set before us." This path is none other than that which all the saints of faith have run before, as described in Hebrews 11. *They've done it; you can too,* is the message.

You may find it strange, but I love it when someone comes to the office to talk to me, pouring out their heart, saying, "Rick, I'm just struggling. I'm doing this sin and I hate it. I need help. I find that I keep doing it and I don't want to. There's something I want to do and I don't do that enough. Am I really even saved? I keep trying and failing!" I generally smile and affirm them: "You know, that's probably the best form of assurance you can find. You're in the race. You're dealing with encumbrances, wrestling with sin. You're trying to do better!"

It's the people who sit around eating "spiritual Doritos" that I'm concerned about. They have all the trappings, but they're lulled into spiritual sleep. They come to church, they go to Bible study, they have their name engraved on their Bible, they've met some Christian leaders at conferences, they're in the church directory. But for all that, they're doing very little throughout the week to repent and to reflect. There's no worship of Jesus. No time to pause and meditate. They're not running.

What about you? Are you running?

Here's the test. Are you tired?

If you're tired, you're probably running. If you feel the weariness from the marathon battle against sin and distraction, you're in it. Until you hear "'Well done, good and faithful slave...enter into the joy of your master'" (Matthew 25:21) at the gates of heaven, this is what you are to be about. If you're not racing,

you're not fighting your sins,

you're not laying aside encumbrances,

you're not running the race with the rest of us.

GET YOUR EYES FIXED

Let's keep this simple. After all, this is a simple book and we're only in the introduction anyway.

Focus on Jesus.

Focusing on Jesus and dealing with sin are not two separate exercises. This passage makes that clear. Runners in the race of faith need to always be "fixing [their] eyes on Jesus" (Hebrews 12:2). If you focus on Christ, you'll see sin and deal with it. If you see your sin rightly, it will make you run to Christ. Put another way, we're to concentrate our faith on Jesus.

Let's keep track of the flow of Hebrews. For all of chapter eleven, faith is pictured as believing God, trusting His Word, understanding the tasks that He called these people to do. While it's true that their obedience was outlined by the law and preached by the prophets, it was still somewhat nebulous compared to what we enjoy. Our faith is not an Old Testament faith. It's a new covenant faith.

Here Jesus is called the "Author and Perfecter" of faith and as such we fix our soul's gaze on Him. Jesus is the one for whom and with whom we should look to finish the course. "The author" means the leader and the founder. Jesus founded the Christian faith and He directs it. The "perfecter" is the one who brings something to a successful conclusion. He's the beginning and the end, the bookends of faith. Notice it doesn't say, "our faith." This is conceptual. He's the Author and the Perfecter of faith in general, having prescribed for all that would follow Him a life of trusting and obeying God rather than the world and their appetites. Second Corinthians 5:7 says, "We walk by faith, not by sight." The world simply reverses that pattern. They walk by sight, enjoying what they can and living by their senses. But we've fixed our eyes on the Son, whom we can see only by faith.

It's important not to miss how this phrase "fixing our eyes on Jesus" highlights His humanity. He too lived by faith! Specifically, Jesus lived by faith as He endured suffering and difficulty and humiliation as a human being. He lived by the same kind of faith that you and I do, as the author of Hebrews highlights earlier in chapters 2 and 4. Jesus gave us an example, and we're to never let His example out of our sight. In all the contingencies of life, we're to be relying on, supported by, and inspired with the faith of Jesus.

If you have ever seen a chameleon up close you know their eyes are different from ours. These amazing creatures, whose eyes are on opposite sides of their heads, can focus each of them on something different. Perhaps in their native habitat this enables them to track both breakfast and lunch at the same time. But God gave that capability to lizards, not to humankind. We cannot, either physically or spiritually with the eyes of faith, bring two different objects into focus at once. As John Owen put it, "A constant view of the glory of Christ will revive our souls and cause our spiritual lives to flourish and thrive. The more we behold the glory of Christ by faith now, the more spiritual and the more heavenly will be the state of our souls. The reason why spiritual life in our souls decays and withers is because we fill our mind with other things.... But when the mind is filled with thoughts of Christ and His glory, these things will be expelled.... This is how our spiritual life will be revived."[4]

Living by faith changes our souls. Laying aside sin and putting on Christ go hand in glove. When our minds are full of other things, they can't be full of Christ and He is tragically eclipsed. You cannot spiritually multitask. For this reason we need to endeavor to turn all of our worldly pursuits into spiritual pursuits. That's why Paul told the Colossians that Jesus is to have first place not *above* everything, but *in* everything (Colossians 1:18). If we fail in this, our very soul decays as our clear vision of Christ is swallowed up in the dead-end quests of the world.

ON A HILL FAR AWAY

So what's the problem? Why don't we fix our eyes on Jesus? Why do we have this persistent wandering vision, so often seeing everything but Jesus clearly? Perhaps it's because we are not motivated by the gospel, the record of what Jesus accomplished on our behalf.

The work that the Author and Perfecter of faith did by faith far supersedes that of the heroes enumerated in Hebrews 11. The author of Hebrews invites us to consider Jesus' mission and the source of His joy as we're looking to Him by faith: "who for the joy set before Him endured the cross, despising the shame, and has sat down at the right hand of the throne of God. For consider Him who has endured such hostility by sinners against Himself, so that you will not grow weary and lose heart" (Hebrews 12:2–3).

Did Jesus take joy in His scourging?

In the rejection and denial of His friends?

In laying His hands out, putting His feet down, to be nailed to a cross?

In being stripped naked and elevated in humiliation?

No, He despised the shame of it all. But Jesus was encouraged knowing what was going to happen immediately after His heart stopped. He would enter the joy of pure fellowship with His Father, unhindered. In a similar way, we take joy as we look forward to that same kind of relationship with the Father, the Son, and the Spirit. Jesus now "has sat down at the right hand of the throne of God" the Father. His work is accomplished.

The simple injunction to us based on this is "consider Him."

Think about Jesus. Let Him be the focus. He has "endured such hostility by sinners against Himself." Only as we do this will we "not grow weary and lose heart." The gospel itself provides the motivation and the stimulation for us to be faithful to it. We must live preaching the gospel to our own hearts.

We should never get tired of thinking about the cross because we can never get tired when thinking about the cross. Jesus, the cross bearer, is both the object of our faith and the great example of living by faith. The cross was not something that happened to Jesus passively, unwillingly, accidentally. He deliberately endured that cross, knowing He had all of heaven's angels ready to rescue Him. Jesus had a cosmic transaction to make, a redemption to accomplish. Consider Him.

GAINING CHRIST

Perhaps you've spent so long admiring the eclipse, you don't remember what it's like to walk in the fullness of the light of Christ. If that's the case, consider this your introduction to a new kind of focus in your Christian life, a bare focus on worshipping Jesus. Here are a few last applications for your journey...

To get very far in this life, you must learn to compare.

Paul had figured this out in Philippians 3:8. He explains, "I count all things to be loss in view of the surpassing value of knowing Christ Jesus my Lord, for whom I have suffered the loss of all things, and count them but rubbish so that I may gain Christ." He compared his accomplishments, his standing as a Jewish leader, and his legacy as a kind of hero for the Judaizers all to Jesus.

This is the ultimate and ever-present challenge for us. Weighing any privilege, blessing, or pleasure in this world against the pleasures and the blessings and the privileges of Jesus. There is no comparison. But you'll never know that until you seriously look at the world and what it has to offer, and deeply look at Jesus and who He is and what He offers.

A second application is related to looking deeply and carefully at Jesus. You must learn to meditate. Slow down and really dig deep into God's Word with the eye of faith. Our lives are moving by so quickly that we can never quite see Jesus apart from the shadows. At some point during each day you need to steep in a passage of Scripture, considering Him that you might gain Him.

As I finish this book the Puritan John Fawcett puts my heart to words perfectly:

> Christ Jesus is the life of all the graces and comforts of a Christian in this world. By the knowledge and contemplation of Him, and of His death in our stead, faith lives, and is strengthened from day to day; all the springs of repentance are opened, and flow freely, when the heart is melted by views of a dying Savior;

love feels the attractive power of its glorious object, and is kindled into a holy flame; sin is mortified; the world is subdued; and the hope of future glory is supported, enlivened, and confirmed, so as to become sure and steadfast, like an anchor of the soul. But without Him, whom having not seen we love, these graces would wither and die, or, to speak more properly, they would have no existence.[5]

Only those in the shadow of the moon experience the phenomenon of a solar eclipse. The brilliance of the sun is not diminished, only obscured. When the moon moves, the radiance returns. And my prayer as we conclude this introduction is that many of you will escape the twilight of tepid religiosity, remove whatever is eclipsing Jesus in your soul, and step into the broad and satisfying daylight of the Son of God, your Lord, Savior, Redeemer, and Friend.

Notes

Chapter 1

1. Robert M. Bowman Jr. and J. Ed Komoszewski, *Putting Jesus in His Place: The Case for the Deity of Christ* (Grand Rapids, MI: Kregel, 2007), 20.

Chapter 2

1. George M. Marsden, *Jonathan Edwards: A Life* (New Haven, CT: Yale University Press, 2003), 220.
2. Ibid., 224.
3. Ibid., 220.
4. Jonathan Edwards, "Sinners in the Hands of an Angry God," in *The Wrath of Almighty God: Jonathan Edwards on God's Judgment Against Sinners*, ed. Don Kistler (Morgan, PA: Soli Deo Gloria Publications, 1996), 72–73.
5. Charles Haddon Spurgeon, "The Blood of the Testament: A Sermon Published on March 14, 1912," in *The Metropolitan Tabernacle Pulpit* (London: Passmore and Alabaster, 1881), 26:629.
6. Edwards, "Sinners," 66.

Chapter 3

1. Percival Lowell, *Mars As the Abode of Life* (New York: Macmillian, 1910), 215.

Chapter 4

1. A. W. Tozer, *The Knowledge of the Holy: The Attributes of God, Their Meaning in the Christian Life* (New York: Harper & Brothers, 1961), 9.

Chapter 5

1. James Montgomery Boice, *The Gospel of John* (Grand Rapids: Baker Books, 2005), 4:1144.
2. Ibid.
3. Thomas Vincent, *The True Christian's Love for the Unseen Christ* (Morgan, PA: Soli Deo Gloria Publications, 1993), 10.
4. Ibid., 66.
5. Jonathan Edwards, *The Religious Affections* (Edinburgh: The Banner of Truth, 1746), 52–53.

Chapter 6

1. Vincent, *Christian's Love*, 127.

Chapter 7

1. John Owen, *Overcoming Sin and Temptation*, ed. Kelly M. Kapic and Justin Taylor (Wheaton, IL: Crossway, 2006), 202.
2. John Piper, introduction to *Overcoming Sin and Temptation*, by John Owen, ed. Kelly M. Kapic and Justin Taylor (Wheaton, IL: Crossway, 2006), 13.
3. Owen, *Overcoming Sin and Temptation*, 282.
4. J. C. Ryle, *Holiness* (Moscow, ID: Charles Nolan Publishers, 2001), 8.
5. Martin Luther, *What Luther Says* (St. Louis, MO: Concordia Publishing House, 1959), 3:1527.

Chapter 9

1. J. C. Ryle, *Knots Untied* (Moscow, ID: Charles Nolan Publishers, 2000), 170.
2. J. C. Ryle, *Practical Religion* (Auburn, MA: Evangelical Press, 2001), 166.
3. Ryle, *Knots Untied*, 187.
4. Jasper Ridley, *Bloody Mary's Martyrs* (New York: Carroll & Graf Publishers, 2001), 1.
5. Ibid., 65.
6. Ibid., 67.
7. J. C. Ryle, *Light from Old Times* (Moscow, ID: Charles Nolan Publishers, 2000), 44.
8. Ibid., 48.
9. Ridley, *Bloody Mary's Martyrs*, 133–37.
10. Ibid., 152.

Chapter 10

1. Kenda Creasy Dean, *Almost Christian: What the Faith of Our Teenagers is Telling the American Church* (Oxford: Oxford University Press, 2010), 3.
2. Ibid., 4.
3. Ibid., 38.
4. John Owen, *The Works of John Owen* (Edinburgh: The Banner of Truth Trust, 1965), 1:164.

Chapter 11

1. Jennifer Yang, "Survivorman fan found dead in Muskoka wilderness," *thestar.com*, March 3, 2010, http://www.thestar.com/news/gta/article/774517--survivorman-fan-found-dead-in-muskoka-wilderness (accessed May 3, 2011).
2. J. C. Ryle, *The Christian Race* (Moscow, ID: Charles Nolan Publishers, 2002), 131.
3. Ibid., 127.
4. John Owen, *The Glory of Christ: Abridged and Made Easy to Read* by R. J. K. Law (Edinburgh: Banner of Truth, 1994; repr., 2000), 167.
5. John Fawcett, *Christ Precious to Those That Believe: A Practical Treatise on Faith and Love* (Whitakers, NC: Positive Action for Christ, 2005), 5.